PSYCHO-ANALYTIC NOTES ON AN AUTOBIOGRAPHICAL ACCOUNT OF A CASE OF PARANOIA (DEMENTIA PARANOIDES)

BY

SIGMUND FREUD

British Library Cataloguing-in-Publication Data
A catalogue record for this book is available from the
British Library

Contents

Sigmund Freud

Sigismund Schlomo Freud was born on 6th May 1856, in the Moravian town of Příbor, now part of the Czech Republic.

Sigmund was the eldest of eight children to Jewish Galician parents, Jacob and Amalia Freud. After Freud's father lost his business as a result of the Panic of 1857, the family were forced to move to Leipzig and then Vienna to avoid poverty. It was in Vienna that the nine-year-old Sigmund enrolled at the Leopoldstädter Kommunal-Realgymnasium before beginning his medical training at the University of Vienna in 1873, at the age of just 17. He studied a variety of subjects, including philosophy, physiology, and zoology, graduating with an MD in 1881.

The following year, Freud began his medical career in Theodor Meynert's psychiatric clinic at the Vienna General Hospital. He worked there until 1886 when he set up in private practice and began specialising in "nervous disorders". In the same year he married Merth Bernays, with whom he had 6 children between 1887 and 1895.

In the period between 1896 and 1901, Freud isolated himself from his colleagues and began work on developing the basics of his psychoanalytic theory. He published *The Interpretation of Dreams*, in 1899, to a lacklustre reception, but continued to produce works such as *The Psychopathology of Everyday Life* (1901) and *Three Essays on the Theory of Sexuality* (1905). He held a weekly meeting at his home known as the "Wednesday Psychological Society" which eventually developed into the Vienna Psycho-Analytic Society. His ideas gained momentum and by the end of the decade his methods were being used internationally by neurologists and psychiatrists.

Freud made a huge and lasting contribution to the field of psychology with many of his methods still being used in modern psychoanalysis. He inspired much discussion on the wealth of theories he produced and the reactions to his works began a century of great psychological investigation.

In 1930 Freud fled Vienna due to rise of Nazism and resided in England until his death from mouth cancer on 23rd September 1939.

PSYCHO-ANALYTIC NOTES ON AN AUTOBIOGRAPHICAL ACCOUNT OF A CASE OF PARANOIA (DEMENTIA PARANOIDES)

The analytic investigation of paranoia presents difficulties of a peculiar nature to physicians who, like myself, are not attached to public institutions. We cannot accept patients suffering from this complaint, or, at all events, we cannot keep them for long, since we cannot offer treatment unless there is some prospect of therapeutic success. It is only in exceptional circumstances, therefore, that I succeed in getting more than a superficial view of the structure of paranoia - when, for instance, the diagnosis (which is not always an easy matter) is uncertain enough to justify an attempt at influencing the patient, or when, in spite of an assured diagnosis, I yield to the entreaties of the patient's relatives and undertake to treat him for a time. Apart from this, of course, I see plenty of cases of paranoia and of dementia praecox, and I learn as much about them as other psychiatrists do about their cases; but that is not enough, as a rule, to lead to any analytic conclusions.

The psycho-analytic investigation of paranoia would be altogether impossible if the patients themselves did not possess the peculiarity of betraying (in a distorted form, it is true) precisely those things which other neurotics keep hidden as a secret. Since paranoics cannot be compelled to overcome their internal resistances, and since in any case they only say what they choose to say, it follows that this is precisely a disorder in which a written report or a printed case history can take the place of personal acquaintance with the patient. For this reason I think it is legitimate to base analytic interpretations upon the case history of a patient suffering from paranoia (or, more precisely, from dementia paranoides) whom I have never seen, but who has written his own case history and brought it before the public in print.

I refer to Dr. jur. Daniel Paul Schreber, formerly Senatspräsident in Dresden, whose book, *Denkwürdigkeiten eines Nervenkranken* [*Memoirs of a Nerve Patient*], was published in 1903, and, if I am rightly informed, aroused considerable interest among psychiatrists. It is possible that Dr. Schreber may still be living to-day and that he may have dissociated himself so far from the delusional system which he put forward in 1903 as to be pained by these notes upon his book. In so far, however, as he still retains his identity with his former personality, I can rely upon the arguments with which he himself - 'a man of superior mental gifts and endowed with an unusual keenness alike of intellect and of observation'[1] - countered the efforts that were made to restrain him from publishing his memoirs: 'I have been at no pains', he writes, 'to close my eyes to the difficulties

4

that would appear to lie in the path of publication, and in particular to the problem of paying due regard to the susceptibilities of certain persons still living. On the other hand, I am of opinion that it might well be to the advantage both of science and of the recognition of religious truths if, during my life-time, qualified authorities were enabled to undertake some examination of my body and to hold some enquiry into my personal experiences. To this consideration all feelings of a personal character must yield.'[2] He declares in another passage that he has decided to keep to his intention of publishing the book, even if the consequence were to be that his physician, Geheimrat Dr. Flechsig of Leipzig, brought an action against him. He urges upon Dr. Flechsig, however, the same considerations that I am now urging upon him himself: 'I trust', he says, 'that even in the case of Geheimrat Prof. Dr. Flechsig any personal susceptibilities that he may feel will be outweighed by a scientific interest in the subject-matter of my memoirs.' (446.)[3]

Though all the passages from the *Denkwürdigkeiten* upon which my interpretations are based will be quoted verbatim in the following pages, I would ask my readers to make themselves acquainted with the book by reading it through at least once beforehand.

[1] This piece of self-portraiture, which is certainly not unjustified, will be found on page 35 of his book.

[2] Preface, iii.

[3] [Throughout this paper figures in brackets with no preceding 'p.' are page references to the original German edition of Schreber's memoirs - *Denkwürdigkeiten eines Nervenkranken*, Leipzig, Oswald Mutze.]

I
CASE HISTORY

'I have suffered twice from nervous disorders', writes Dr. Schreber, 'and each time as a result of mental overstrain. This was due on the first occasion to my standing as a candidate for election to the Reichstag while I was Landgerichtsdirektor at Chemnitz, and on the second occasion to the very heavy burden of work that fell upon my shoulders when I entered on my new duties as Senatspräsident in the Oberlandesgericht in Dresden.' (34.)

Dr. Schreber's first illness began in the autumn of 1884, and by the end of 1885 he had completely recovered. During this period he spent six months in Flechsig's clinic, and the latter, in a formal report which he drew up at a later date, described the disorder as an attack of severe hypochondria. Dr. Schreber assures us that this illness ran its course 'without the occurrence of any incidents bordering upon the sphere of the supernatural'. (35.)

Neither the patient's own account, nor the reports of the physicians which are reprinted at the end of his book, tell us enough about his previous history or his personal circumstances. I am not even in a position to give the patient's age at the time of his illness, though the high judicial position which he had attained before his second illness establishes some sort of lower limit. We learn that Dr. Schreber had been married long before the time of his 'hypochondria'. 'The gratitude of my wife', he writes, 'was perhaps even more heartfelt; for she revered Professor Flechsig as the man who had restored her husband to her, and hence it was that for years she kept his portrait standing upon her writing-table.' (36.) And in the same place: 'After my recovery from my first illness I spent eight years with my wife - years, upon the whole, of great happiness, rich in outward honours, and only clouded from time to time by the oft repeated disappointment of our hope that we might be blessed with children.'

In June, 1893, he was notified of his prospective appointment as Senatspräsident, and he took up his duties on the first of October of the same year. Between these two dates[1] he had some dreams, though it was not until later that he came to attach any importance to them. He dreamt two or three times that his old nervous disorder had come back; and this made him as miserable in the dream as the discovery that it was only a dream made him happy when he woke up. Once, in the early hours of the morning, moreover, while he was in a state between sleeping and waking, the idea occurred to him 'that after all it really must be very nice to be a woman submitting to the act of copulation'. (36.) This idea was one which he would have rejected with the greatest indignation if he had been fully conscious.

8

Psycho-Analytic Notes on an Autobiographical Account of a Case of Paranoia (Dementia Paranoides)

The second illness set in at the end of October 1893 with a torturing bout of sleeplessness. This forced him to return to the Flechsig clinic, where, however, his condition grew rapidly worse. The further course of the illness is described in a Report drawn up subsequently by the director of the Sonnenstein Asylum: 'At the commencement of his residence there[2] he expressed more hypochondriacal ideas, complained that he had softening of the brain, that he would soon be dead, etc. But ideas of persecution were already finding their way into the clinical picture, based upon sensory illusions which, however, seemed only to appear sporadically at first; while simultaneously a high degree of hyperaesthesia was observable - great sensitiveness to light and noise. - Later, the visual and auditory illusions became much more frequent, and, in conjunction with coenaesthetic disturbances, dominated the whole of his feeling and thought. He believed that he was dead and decomposing, that he was suffering from the plague; he asserted that his body was being handled in all kinds of revolting ways; and, as he himself declares to this day, he went through worse horrors than any one could have imagined, and all on behalf of a holy purpose. The patient was so much pre-occupied with these pathological experiences that he was inaccessible to any other impression and would sit perfectly rigid and motionless for hours (hallucinatory stupor). On the other hand, they tortured him to such a degree that he longed for death. He made repeated attempts at drowning himself in his bath, and asked to be given the "cyanide that was intended for him". His delusional ideas gradually assumed a mystical and religious character; he was in direct communication with God, he was the plaything of devils, he saw "miraculous apparitions", he heard "holy music", and in the end he even came to believe that he was living in another world.' (380.)

[1] And therefore before he could have been affected by the overwork caused by his new post, to which he attributes his illness.

[2] In Professor Flechsig's clinic at Leipzig.

It may be added that there were certain people by whom he thought he was being persecuted and injured, and upon whom he poured abuse. The most prominent of these was his former physician, Flechsig, whom he called a 'soul-murderer'; and he used to call out over and over again: '*Little* Flechsig!' putting a sharp stress upon the first word (383). He was moved from Leipzig, and, after a short interval spent in another institution, was brought in June 1894 to the Sonnenstein Asylum, near Pirna, where he remained until his disorder assumed its final shape. In the course of the next few years the clinical picture altered in a manner which can best be described in the words of Dr. Weber, the director of the asylum.

'I need not enter any further into the details of the course of the disease. I must, however, draw attention to the manner in which, as time went on, the initial comparatively acute psychosis, which had directly involved the patient's entire mental life and deserved the name of "hallucinatory insanity", developed more and more clearly (one might almost say crystallized out) into the paranoic clinical picture that we have before us to-day.' (385.) The fact was that, on the one hand, he had developed an ingenious delusional structure, in which we have every reason to be interested, while, on the other hand, his personality had been reconstructed and now showed itself, except for a few isolated disturbances, capable of meeting the demands of everyday life.

Dr. Weber, in his Report of 1899, makes the following remarks: 'It thus appears that at the present time, apart from certain obvious psychomotor symptoms which cannot fail to strike even the superficial observer as being pathological, Herr Senatspräsident Dr. Schreber shows no signs of confusion or of psychical inhibition, nor is his intelligence noticeably impaired. His mind is collected, his memory is excellent, he has at his disposal a very considerable store of knowledge (not merely upon legal questions, but in many other fields), and he is able to reproduce it in a connected train of thought. He takes an interest in following events in the world of politics, science and art, etc., and is constantly occupied with such matters . . . and an observer who was uninstructed upon his general condition would scarcely notice anything peculiar in these directions. In spite of all this, however, the patient

11

is full of ideas of pathological origin, which have formed themselves into a complete system; they are more or less fixed, and seem to be inaccessible to correction by means of any objective appreciation and judgement of the external facts.' (305-6.)

Thus the patient's condition had undergone a great change, and he now considered himself capable of carrying on an independent existence. He accordingly took appropriate steps with a view to regaining control over his own affairs and to securing his discharge from the asylum. Dr. Weber set himself to prevent the fulfilment of these intentions and drew up reports in opposition to them. Nevertheless, in his Report dated 1900, he felt obliged to give this appreciative account of the patient's character and conduct: 'Since for the last nine months Herr Präsident Schreber has taken his meals daily at my family board, I have had the most ample opportunities of conversing with him upon every imaginable topic, Whatever the subject was that came up for discussion (apart, of course, from his delusional ideas), whether it concerned events in the field of administration and law, of politics, art, literature or social life - in short, whatever the topic, Dr. Schreber gave evidence of a lively interest, a well-informed mind, a good memory, and a sound judgement; his ethical outlook, moreover, was one which it was impossible not to endorse. So, too, in his lighter talk with the ladies of the party, he was both courteous and affable, and when he touched upon matters in a more humorous vein he invariably displayed tact and decorum. Never once, during these innocent talks round the dining-table, did he introduce subjects which should more properly have been raised at a medical consultation.' (397-8.) Indeed, on one occasion during this period when a business question arose which involved the interests of his whole family, he entered into it in a manner which showed both his technical knowledge and his common sense (401 and 510).

In the numerous applications to the courts, by which Dr. Schreber endeavoured to regain his liberty, he did not in the least disavow his delusions or make any secret of his intention of publishing the *Denkwürdigkeiten*. On the contrary, he dwelt upon the importance of his ideas to religious thought, and upon their invulnerability to the attacks of modern science; but at the same time he laid stress upon the 'absolute harmlessness' (430) of all the actions which, as he was aware, his delusions obliged him to perform. Such, indeed, were his acumen and the cogency of his logic that finally, and in spite of his being an acknowledged paranoic, his efforts were crowned with success. In July, 1902, Dr. Schreber's civil rights were restored, and in the following year his *Denkwürdigkeiten eines Nervenkranken* appeared, though in a censored form and with many valuable portions omitted.

The Court Judgement that gave Dr. Schreber back
his liberty summarizes the content of his delusional system
in a few sentences: 'He believed that he had a mission to
redeem the world and to restore it to its lost state of bliss.
This, however, he could only bring about if he were first
transformed from a man into a woman.' (475.)

For a more detailed account of his delusions as they
appeared in their final shape we may turn to Dr. Weber's
Report of 1899: 'The culminating point of the patient's
delusional system is his belief that he has a mission to
redeem the world, and to restore mankind to their lost
state of bliss. He was called to this task, so he asserts, by
direct inspiration from God, just as we are taught that the
Prophets were; for nerves in a condition of great excitement,
as his were for a long time, have precisely the property of
exerting an attraction upon God - though this is touching
on matters which human speech is scarcely, if at all, capable
of expressing, since they lie entirely outside the scope of
human experience and, indeed, have been revealed to him
alone. The most essential part of his mission of redemption is
that it must be preceded by his *transformation into a woman*.
It is not to be supposed that he *wishes* to be transformed into
a woman; it is rather a question of a "must" based upon the
Order of Things, which there is no possibility of his evading,
much as he would personally prefer to remain in his own
honourable and masculine station in life. But neither he

nor the rest or mankind can regain the life beyond except
by his being transformed into a woman (a process which
may occupy many years or even decades) by means of divine
miracles. He himself, of this he is convinced, is the only
object upon which divine miracles are worked, and he is
thus the most remarkable human being who has ever lived
upon earth. Every hour and every minute for years he has
experienced these miracles in his body, and he has had them
confirmed by the voices that have conversed with him.
During the first years of his illness certain of his bodily
organs suffered such destructive injuries as would inevitably
have led to the death of any other man: he lived for a long
time without a stomach, without intestines, almost without
lungs, with a torn oesophagus, without a bladder, and with
shattered ribs, he used sometimes to swallow part of his own
larynx with his food, etc. But divine miracles ("rays") always
restored what had been destroyed, and therefore, as long as
he remains a man, he is altogether immortal. These alarming
phenomena have ceased long ago, and his "femaleness" has
become prominent instead. This is a matter of a process of
development which will probably require decades, if not
centuries, for its completion, and it is unlikely that anyone
now living will survive to see the end of it. He has a feeling
that enormous numbers of "female nerves" have already
passed over into his body, and out of them a new race of
men will proceed, through a process of direct impregnation

by God. Not until then, it seems, will he be able to die a natural death, and, along with the rest of mankind, will he regain a state of bliss. In the meantime not only the sun, but trees and birds, which are in the nature of "bemiracled residues of former human souls", speak to him in human accents, and miraculous things happen everywhere around him.' (386-8.)

The interest felt by the practical psychiatrist in such delusional formations as these is, as a rule, exhausted when once he has ascertained the character of the products of the delusion and has formed an estimate of their influence on the patient's general behaviour: in his case marvelling is not the beginning of understanding. The psycho-analyst, in the light of his knowledge of the psychoneuroses, approaches the subject with a suspicion that even thought-structures so extraordinary as these and so remote from our common modes of thinking are nevertheless derived from the most general and comprehensible impulses of the human mind; and he would be glad to discover the motives of such a transformation as well as the manner in which it has been accomplished. With this aim in view, he will wish to go more deeply into the details of the delusion and into the history of its development.

(*a*) The medical officer lays stress upon two points as being of chief importance: the patient's *assumption of the role of Redeemer*, and his *transformation into a woman*. The

Redeemer delusion is a phantasy that is familiar to us through
the frequency with which it forms the nucleus of religious
paranoia. The additional factor, which makes the redemption
dependent upon the man being previously transformed into
a woman, is unusual and in itself bewildering, since it shows
such a wide divergence from the historical myth which the
patient's phantasy is setting out to reproduce. It is natural
to follow the medical report in assuming that the motive
force of this delusional complex was the patient's ambition
to play the part of Redeemer, and that his *emasculation* was
only entitled to be regarded as a means for achieving that
end. Even though this may appear to be true of his delusion
in its final form, a study of the *Denkwürdigkeiten* compels
us to take a very different view of the matter. For we learn
that the idea of being transformed into a woman (that is, of
being emasculated) was the primary delusion, that he began
by regarding that act as constituting a serious injury and
persecution, and that it only became related to his playing the
part of Redeemer in a secondary way. There can be no doubt,
moreover, that originally he believed that the transformation
was to be effected for the purpose of sexual abuse and not so
as to serve higher designs. The position may be formulated
by saying that a sexual delusion of persecution was later on
converted in the patient's mind into a religious delusion
of grandeur. The part of persecutor was at first assigned to

Professor Flechsig, the physician in whose charge he was; later, his place was taken by God Himself.

I will quote the relevant passages from the *Denkwürdigkeiten* in full: 'In this way a conspiracy against me was brought to a head (in about March or April, 1894). Its object was to contrive that, when once my nervous complaint had been recognized as incurable or assumed to be so, I should be handed over to a certain person in a particular manner: my soul was to be delivered up to him, but my body - owing to a misapprehension of what I have described above as the purpose underlying the Order of Things - was to be transformed into a female body: and as such surrendered to the person in question[1] with a view to sexual abuse, and was then simply to be "left on one side" - that is to say, no doubt, given over to corruption.' (56.)

'It was, moreover, perfectly natural that from the human standpoint (which was the one by which at that time I was still chiefly governed) I should regard Professor Flechsig or his soul as my only true enemy - at a later date there was also the von W. soul, about which I shall have more to say presently - and that I should look upon God Almighty as my natural ally. I merely fancied that He was in great straits as regards Professor Flechsig, and consequently felt myself bound to support him by every conceivable means, even to the length of sacrificing myself. It was not until very much later that the idea forced itself upon my mind that

God Himself had played the part of accomplice, if not of instigator, in the plot whereby my soul was to be murdered and my body used like a strumpet. I may say, in fact, that this idea has in part become clearly conscious to me only in the course of writing the present work.' (59.)

'Every attempt at murdering my soul, or at emasculating me for purposes *contrary to the Order of Things* (that is, for the gratification of the sexual appetites of a human individual), or later at destroying my understanding - every such attempt has come to nothing. From this apparently unequal struggle between one weak man and God Himself, I have emerged as the victor - though not without undergoing much bitter suffering and privation - because the Order of Things stands upon my side.' (61.)

In a footnote attached to the words *'contrary to the Order of Things'* in the above passage, the author foreshadows the subsequent transformation in his delusion of emasculation and in his relation to God: 'I shall show later on that emasculation for quite another purpose - a purpose *in consonance with the Order of Things* - is within the bounds of possibility, and, indeed, that it may quite probably afford the solution of the conflict.'

[1] It is shown from the context in this and other passages that 'the person in question' who was to practise this abuse was none other than Flechsig. (See below.)

These statements are of decisive importance in determining the view we are to take of the delusion of emasculation and in thus giving us a general understanding of the case. It may be added that the 'voices' which the patient heard never treated his transformation into a woman as anything but a sexual disgrace, which gave them an excuse for jeering at him. 'Rays of God[1] not infrequently thought themselves entitled to mock at me by calling me "Miss[2] Schreber", in allusion to the emasculation which, it was alleged, I was about to undergo.' (127.) Or they would say: 'So *this* sets up to have been a Senatspräsident, this person who lets himself be f--d!'[3] Or again: 'Don't you feel ashamed in front of your wife?'

That the emasculation phantasy was of a primary nature and originally independent of the Redeemer *motif* becomes still more probable when we recollect the 'idea' which, as I mentioned on an earlier page, occurred to him while he was half asleep, to the effect that it must be nice to be a woman submitting to the act of copulation (36.) This phantasy appeared during the incubation period of his illness, and before he had begun to feel the effects of overwork in Dresden.

Schreber himself gives the month of November, 1895, as the date at which the connection was established between the emasculation phantasy and the Redeemer idea and the way thus paved for his becoming reconciled to the former.

'Now, however,' he writes, 'I became clearly aware that the
Order of Things imperatively demanded my emasculation,
whether I personally liked it or no, and that no *reasonable*
course lay open to me but to reconcile myself to the
thought of being transformed into a woman. The further
consequence of my emasculation could, of course, only be
my impregnation by divine rays to the end that a new race
of men might be created.' (177.)

[1] The 'rays of God', as we shall see, are identical with the voices
which talked the 'basic language'.

[2] [In English in the original.]

[3] I reproduce this omission from the *Denkwürdigkeiten*, just as I
do all the peculiarities of their author's way of writing. I myself
should have found no reason for being so shamefaced over a
serious matter.

The idea of being transformed into a woman was the
salient feature and the earliest germ of his delusional system.
It also proved to be the one part of it that persisted after his
cure, and the one part that was able to retain a place in his
behaviour in real life after he had recovered. 'The *only thing*
which could appear unreasonable in the eyes of other people
is the fact, already touched upon in the expert's report, that
I am sometimes to be found standing before the mirror or
elsewhere with the upper portion of my body bared, and
wearing sundry feminine adornments, such as ribbons, false
necklaces, and the like. This only occurs, I may add, when

I am *by myself*, and never, at least so far as I am able to avoid it, in the presence of other people.' (429.) The Herr Senatspräsident confesses to this frivolity at a date (July, 1901) at which he was already in a position to express very aptly the completeness of his recovery in the region of practical life: 'I have now long been aware that the persons I see about me are not "cursorily improvised men" but real people, and that I must therefore behave towards them as a reasonable man is used to behave towards his fellows.' (409.) In contrast to the way in which he put his emasculation phantasy into action, the patient never took any steps towards inducing people to recognize his mission as Redeemer, beyond the publication of his *Denkwürdigkeiten*.

(*b*) The attitude of our patient towards *God* is so singular and so full of internal contradictions that it requires more than a little faith to persist in the belief that there is nevertheless 'method' in his 'madness'. With the help of what Dr. Schreber tells us in the *Denkwürdigkeiten*, we must now endeavour to arrive at a more exact view of his theologico-psychological system, and we must expound his opinions concerning *nerves, the state of bliss, the divine hierarchy*, and *the attributes of God*, in their manifest (delusional) nexus. At every point in his theory we shall be struck by the astonishing mixture of the commonplace and the clever, of what has been borrowed and what is original.

Psycho-Analytic Notes on an Autobiographical Account of a Case of Paranoia (Dementia Paranoides)

The human soul is comprised in the *nerves* of the body. These are to be conceived of as structures of extraordinary fineness, comparable to the finest thread. Some of these nerves are suited only for the reception of sense-perceptions, while others (*the nerves of understanding*) carry out all the functions of the mind; and in this connection it is to be noticed that *each single nerve of understanding represents a person's entire mental individuality*, and that the presence of a greater or lesser number of nerves of understanding has no influence except upon the length of time during which the mind can retain its impressions.[1]

Whereas men consist of bodies and nerves, God is from His very nature nothing but nerve. But the nerves of God are not, as is the case with human bodies, present in limited numbers, but are infinite or eternal. They possess all the properties of human nerves to an enormously intensified degree. In their creative capacity - that is, their power of turning themselves into every imaginable object in the created world - they are known as *rays*. There is an intimate relation between God and the starry heaven and the sun.[2]

[1] The words in which Schreber states this theory are italicized by him, and he adds a footnote, in which he insists that it can be used as an explanation of heredity: 'The male semen', he declares, 'contains a nerve belonging to the father, and it unites with a nerve taken from the mother's body to form a new entity.' (7.) Here, therefore, we find a quality properly belonging to

23

the spermatozoon transferred on to the nerves, which makes it
probable that Schreber's 'nerves' are derived from the sphere of
ideas connected with sexuality. It not infrequently happens in
the *Denkwürdigkeiten* that an incidental note upon some piece of
delusional theory gives us the desired indication of the genesis of
the delusion and so of its meaning.

[2] In this connection see my discussion below on the significance
of the sun. - The comparison between (or rather the
condensation of) nerves and rays may well have been based on
the linear extension which they have in common. The ray-nerves,
by the way, are no less creative than the spermatozoon-nerves.

When the work of creation was finished, God withdrew
to an immense distance (10-11 and 252) and, in general,
resigned the world to its own laws. He limited His activities
to drawing up to Himself the souls of the dead. It was only
in exceptional instances that He would enter into relations
with particular, highly gifted persons,[1] or would intervene
by means of a miracle in the destinies of the world. God does
not have any regular communication with human souls, in
accordance with the Order of Things, till after death.[2] When
a man dies, his spiritual parts (that is, his nerves) undergo
a process of purification before being finally reunited with
God Himself as 'fore-courts of Heaven'. Thus it comes about
that everything moves in an eternal round, which lies at the
basis of the Order of Things. In creating anything, God is
parting with a portion of Himself, or is giving a portion of

His nerves a different shape. The apparent loss which He thus sustains is made good when, after hundreds and thousands of years, the nerves of dead men, that have entered the state of bliss, once more accrue to Him as 'fore-courts of Heaven' (18 and 19 *n.*).

Souls that have passed through the process of purification enter into the enjoyment of a *state of bliss*.[3] In the meantime they have lost some of their individual consciousness, and have become fused together with other souls into higher unities. Important souls, such as those of men like Goethe, Bismarck, etc., may have to retain their sense of identity for hundreds of years to come, before they too can become resolved into higher soul-complexes, such as 'Jehovah rays' in the case of ancient Jewry: or 'Zoroaster rays' in the case of ancient Persia. In the course of their purification 'souls learn the language which is spoken by God himself, the so-called "basic language", a vigorous though somewhat antiquated German, which is especially characterized by its great wealth of euphemisms'.4 (13.)

[1] In the 'basic language' (see below) this is described as 'making a nerve-connection with them'.

[2] We shall find later that certain criticisms against God are based on this fact.

[3] This consists essentially in a feeling of voluptuousness (see below).

4 On one single occasion during his illness the patient was
vouchsafed the privilege of seeing, with his spiritual eyes, God
Almighty clear and undisguised before him. On that occasion
God uttered what was a very current word in the basic language,
and a forcible though not an amiable one - the word 'Slut!'
(136). [In German '*Luder*'. This term of abuse is occasionally
applied to males, though much more often to females.]

God Himself is not a simple entity. 'Above the
"fore-courts of Heaven" hovered God Himself, who, in
contradistinction to these "anterior realms of God", was also
described as the "posterior realms of God". The posterior
realms of God were, and still are, divided in a strange
manner into two parts, so that a lower God (Ahriman)
was differentiated from an upper God (Ormuzd).' (19.) As
regards the significance of this division Schreber can tell
us no more than that the lower God was more especially
attached to the peoples of a dark race (the Semites) and the
upper God to those of a fair race (the Aryans); nor would
it be reasonable, in such sublime matters, to expect more of
human knowledge. Nevertheless, we are also told that 'in
spite of the fact that in certain respects God Almighty forms
a unity, the lower and the upper God must be regarded as
separate Beings, each of which possesses its own particular
egoism and its own particular instinct of self-preservation,
even in relation to the other, and each of which is therefore
constantly endeavouring to thrust itself in front of the other'

(140 *n.*). Moreover, the two divine Beings behaved in quite different ways towards the unlucky Schreber during the acute stage of his illness.[1]

In the days before his illness Senatspräsident Schreber had been a doubter in religious matters (29 and 64); he had never been able to persuade himself into a firm belief in the existence of a personal God. Indeed, he adduces this fact about his earlier life as an argument in favour of the complete reality of his delusions.[2] But any one who reads the account which follows of the character-traits of Schreber's God will have to allow that the transformation effected by the paranoic disorder was no very fundamental one, and that in the Redeemer of to-day much remains of the doubter of yesterday.

[1] A footnote on page 20 leads us to suppose that a passage in Byron's *Manfred* may have determined Schreber's choice of the names of Persian divinities. We shall later come upon further evidence of the influence of this poem on him.

[2] 'That it was simply a matter of illusions seems to me to be *in my case*, from the very nature of things, psychologically unthinkable. For illusions of holding communication with God or with departed souls can properly only arise in the minds of persons who, before falling into their condition of pathological nervous excitement, already have a firm belief in God and in the immortality of the soul. *This was not by any means so, however,*

in my case, as has been explained at the beginning of this chapter.'
(79.)

For there is a flaw in the Order of Things, as a result of which the existence of God Himself seems to be endangered. Owing to circumstances which are incapable of further explanation, the nerves of *living* men, especially when in a condition of *intense excitement*, may exercise such a powerful attraction upon the nerves of God that He cannot get free from them again, and thus His own existence may be threatened (11). This exceedingly rare occurrence took place in Schreber's case and involved him in the greatest sufferings. The instinct of self-preservation was aroused in God (30), and it then became evident that God was far removed from the perfection ascribed to him by religions. Through the whole of Schreber's book there runs the bitter complaint that God, being only accustomed to communication with the dead, *does not understand living men.*

'In this connection, however, a *fundamental misunderstanding* prevails, which has since run through my whole life like a scarlet thread. It is based precisely upon the fact that, *in accordance with the Order of Things, God really knows nothing about living men* and did not need to know; consonantly with the Order of Things, He needed only to have communication with corpses.' (55.) - 'This state of things . . . I am convinced, is once more to be brought into connection with the fact that God was, if I may so express it, quite incapable of dealing with living men, and was only accustomed to communicate with corpses, or at most with men as they lay asleep (that is, in their dreams).' (141.) - 'I myself feel inclined to exclaim: "*Incredibile scriptu!*" Yet it is all literally true, however difficult it may be for other people to grasp the idea of God's complete inability to judge living men correctly, and however long I myself took to accustom myself to this idea after my innumerable observations upon the subject.' (246.)

But as a result of God's misunderstanding of living men it was possible for Him Himself to become the instigator of the plot against Schreber, to take him for an idiot, and to subject him to these severe ordeals (264). To avoid being set down as an idiot, he submitted himself to an extremely burdensome system of 'enforced thinking'. For 'every time that my intellectual activities ceased, God jumped to the conclusion that my mental faculties were extinct and that the destruction of my understanding (the idiocy), for which He was hoping, had actually set in, and that a withdrawal had now become possible' (206).

The behaviour of God in the matter of the urge to evacuate (or 'sh--') rouses him to a specially high pitch of indignation. The passage is so characteristic that I will quote it in full. But to make it clear I must first explain that both the miracles and the voices proceed from God, that is, from the divine rays.

'Although it will necessitate my touching upon an unsavoury subject, I must devote a few more words to the question that I have just quoted ("Why don't you sh--?") on account of the typical character of the whole business. The need for evacuation, like all else that has to do with my body, is evoked by a miracle. It is brought about by my faeces being forced forwards (and sometimes backwards again) in my intestines; and if, owing to there having already been an evacuation, enough material is not present, then such small remains as there may still be of the contents of my intestines are smeared over my anal orifice. This occurrence is a miracle performed by the upper God, and it is repeated several dozens of times at the least every day. It is associated with an idea which is utterly incomprehensible to human beings and can only be accounted for by God's complete ignorance of living man as an organism. According to this idea "sh--ing" is in a certain sense the final act; that is to say, when once the urge to sh-- has been miracled up, the aim of destroying the understanding is achieved and a final withdrawal of the rays becomes possible. To get to the bottom of the origin of this idea, we must suppose, as it seems to me, that there is a misapprehension in connection with the symbolic meaning of the act of evacuation, a notion, in fact, that any one who has been in such a relation as I have with divine rays is to some extent entitled to sh-- upon the whole world.

'But now what follows reveals the full perfidy[1] of the policy that has been pursued towards me. Almost every time the need for evacuation was miracled up in me, some other person in my vicinity was sent (by having his nerves stimulated for that purpose) to the lavatory, in order to prevent my evacuating. This is a phenomenon which I have observed for years and upon such countless occasions - thousands of them - and with such regularity, as to exclude any possibility of its being attributable to chance. And thereupon comes the question: "Why don't you sh--?" to which the brilliant repartee is made that I am "so stupid or something". The pen well-nigh shrinks from recording so monumental a piece of absurdity as that God, blinded by His ignorance of human nature, can positively go to such lengths as to suppose that there can exist a man too stupid to do what every animal can do - too stupid to be able to sh--. When, upon the occasion of such an urge, I actually succeed in evacuating - and as a rule, since I nearly always find the lavatory engaged, I use a pail for the purpose - the process is always accompanied by the generation of an exceedingly strong feeling of spiritual voluptuousness. For the relief from the pressure caused by the presence of the faeces in the intestines produces a sense of intense well-being in the nerves of voluptuousness; and the same is equally true of making water. For this reason, even down to the present day, while I am passing stool or making water, all the rays are always without exception united; for this very reason, whenever I address myself to these natural functions, an attempt is invariably made, though as a rule in vain, to miracle backwards the urge to pass stool and to make water.'[2] (225-7.)

[1] In a footnote at this point the author endeavours to mitigate the harshness of the word 'perfidy' by a reference to one of his arguments in justification of God. These will be discussed presently.

[2] This confession to a pleasure in the excretory processes, which we have learnt to recognize as one of the auto-erotic components of infantile sexuality, may be compared with the remarks made by little Hans in my 'Analysis of a Phobia in a Five-year-old Boy'.

Furthermore, this singular God of Schreber's is incapable of learning anything by experience: 'Owing to some quality or other inherent in his nature, it seems to be impossible for God to derive any lessons for the future from the experience thus gained.' (186.) He can therefore go on repeating the same tormenting ordeals and miracles and voices, without alteration, year after year, until He inevitably becomes a laughing-stock to the victim of His persecutions.

'The consequence is that, now that the miracles have to a great extent lost the power which they formerly possessed of producing terrifying effects, God strikes me above all, in almost everything that happens to me, as being ridiculous or childish. As regards my own behaviour, this often results in my being obliged in self-defence to play the part of a scoffer

at God, and even, on occasion, to scoff at Him aloud.'
(333.)[1]

This critical and rebellious attitude towards God
is, however, opposed in Schreber's mind by an energetic
counter-current, which finds expression in many places:
'But here again I must most emphatically declare that this is
nothing more than an episode, which will, I hope, terminate
at the latest with my decease, and that the right of scoffing
at God belongs in consequence to me alone and not to other
men. For them He remains the almighty creator of Heaven
and earth, the first cause of all things, and the salvation of
their future, to whom - not withstanding that a few of the
conventional religious ideas may require revision - worship
and the deepest reverence are due.' (333-4.)

Repeated attempts are therefore made to find a
justification for God's behaviour to the patient. In these
attempts, which display as much ingenuity as every other
theodicy, the explanation is based now upon the general
nature of souls, and now upon the necessity for self-
preservation under which God lay, and upon the misleading
influence of the Flechsig soul (60-1 and 160). In general,
however, the illness is looked upon as a struggle between
Schreber the man and God, in which victory lies with the
man, weak though he is, because the Order of Things is on
his side (61).

Psycho-Analytic Notes on an Autobiographical Account of a Case of Paranoia (Dementia Paranoides)

The medical report might easily lead us to suppose that Schreber exhibited the everyday form of Redeemer phantasy, in which the patient believes he is the son of God, destined to save the world from its misery or from the destruction that is threatening it, and so on. It is for this reason that I have been careful to present in detail the peculiarities of Schreber's relation to God. The significance of this relation for the rest of mankind is only rarely alluded to in the *Denkwürdigkeiten* and not until the last phase of his delusional formation. It consists essentially in the fact that no one who dies can enter the state of bliss so long as the greater part of the rays of God are absorbed in his (Schreber's) person, owing to his powers of attraction (32). It is only at a very late stage, too, that his identification with Jesus Christ makes an undisguised appearance (338 and 431).

No attempt at explaining Schreber's case will have any chance of being correct which does not take into account these peculiarities in his conception of God, this mixture of reverence and rebelliousness in his attitude towards Him.

[1] Even in the basic language it occasionally happened that God was not the abuser but the abused. For instance: 'Deuce take it! What a thing to have to say - that God lets himself be f--d!' (194.)

I will now turn to another subject, which is closely related to God, namely, the *state of bliss*. This is also spoken of by Schreber as 'the life beyond' to which the human soul is raised after death by the process of purification. He describes it as a state of uninterrupted enjoyment, bound up with the contemplation of God. This is not very original, but on the other hand it is surprising to learn that Schreber makes a distinction between a male and a female state of bliss.[1] 'The male state of bliss was superior to the female, which seems to have consisted chiefly in an uninterrupted feeling of voluptuousness.' (18.) In other passages this coincidence between the state of bliss and voluptuousness is expressed in plainer language and without reference to sex-distinction; and moreover that element of the state of bliss which consists in the contemplation of God is not further discussed. Thus, for instance: 'The nature of the nerves of God, is such that the state of bliss . . . is accompanied by a very intense sensation of voluptuousness, even though it does not consist exclusively of it.' (51.) And again: 'Voluptuousness may be regarded as a fragment of the state of bliss given in advance, as it were, to men and other living creatures.' (281.) So the state of heavenly bliss is to be understood as being in its essence an intensified continuation of sensual pleasure upon earth!

This view of the state of bliss was far from being an element in Schreber's delusion that originated in the first stages of his illness and was later eliminated as being incompatible with the rest. So late as in the Statement of his Case, drawn up by the patient for the Appeal Court in July,

1901, he emphasizes as one of his greatest discoveries the fact 'that voluptuousness stands in a close relationship (not hitherto perceptible to the rest of mankind) to the state of bliss enjoyed by departed spirits'.[2]

[1] It would be much more in keeping with the wish-fulfilment offered by the life beyond that in it we shall at last be free from the difference between the sexes.

Und jene himmlischen Gestalten

sie fragen nicht nach Mann und Weib.

[And those calm shining sons of morn

They ask not who is maid or boy.]

[2] The possibility of this discovery of Schreber's having a deeper meaning is discussed below.

We shall find, indeed, that this 'close relationship' is the rock upon which the patient builds his hopes of an eventual reconciliation with God and of his sufferings being brought to an end. The rays of God abandon their hostility as soon as they are certain that in becoming absorbed into his body they will experience spiritual voluptuousness (133); God Himself demands that He shall be able to find voluptuousness in him (283), and threatens him with the withdrawal of His rays if he neglects to cultivate voluptuousness and cannot offer God what He demands (320).

This surprising sexualization of the state of heavenly bliss suggests the possibility that Schreber's concept of the state of bliss is derived from a condensation of the two principal meanings of the German word '*selig*' - namely, 'dead' and 'sensually happy'.[1] But this instance of sexualization will also give us occasion to examine the patient's general attitude to the erotic side of life and to questions of sexual indulgence. For we psycho-analysts have hitherto supported the view that the roots of every nervous and mental disorder are chiefly to be found in the patient's sexual life - some of us merely upon empirical grounds, others influenced in addition by theoretical considerations.

[1] Extreme instances of the two uses of the word are to be found in the phrase '

mein seliger Vater' ['my late father'] and in these lines from the duet in *Don Giovanni*:

Ja, dein zu sein auf ewig,

wie selig werd' ich sein.

[Ah, to be thine for ever -

How blissful I should be!]

But the fact that the same word should be used in our language in two such different situations cannot be without significance.

The samples of Schreber's delusions that have already been given enable us without more ado to dismiss the suspicion that it might be precisely this paranoid disorder which would turn out to be the 'negative case' which has so long been sought for - a case in which sexuality plays only a very minor part. Schreber himself speaks again and again as though he shared our prejudice. He is constantly talking in the same breath of 'nervous disorder' and erotic lapses, as though the two things were inseparable.[1]

Before his illness Senatspräsident Schreber had been a man of strict morals: 'Few people', he declares, and I see no reason to doubt his assertion, 'can have been brought up upon such strict moral principles as I was, and few people, all through their lives, can have exercised (especially in sexual matters) a self-restraint conforming so closely to those principles as I may say of myself that I have done.' (281.) After the severe spiritual struggle, of which the phenomena of his illness were the outward signs, his attitude towards the erotic side of life was altered. He had come to see that the cultivation of voluptuousness was incumbent upon him as a duty, and that it was only by discharging this duty that he could end the grave conflict which had broken out within him - or, as he thought, about him. Voluptuousness, so the voices assured him, had become 'God-fearing' and he could only regret that he was not able to devote himself to its cultivation the whole day long.[2] (285.)

[1] 'When moral corruption ("voluptuous excesses") or perhaps nervous disorder had taken a strong enough hold upon the whole population of any terrestrial body', then, thinks Schreber, bearing in mind the Biblical stories of Sodom and Gomorrah, the Deluge, etc., the world in question might come to a catastrophic end (52). - '[A rumour] sowed fear and terror among men,

wrecked the foundations of religion, and spread abroad general nervous disorders and immorality, so that devastating pestilences have descended upon mankind.' (91.) - 'Thus it seems probable that by a "Prince of Hell" the souls meant the uncanny Power that was able to develop in a sense hostile to God as a result of moral depravity among men or of a general state of excessive nervous excitement following upon over-civilization.' (163.)

[2] In connection with his delusions he writes: '*This attraction, however, lost its terrors for the nerves in question, if, and in so far as, upon entering my body, they encountered a feeling of spiritual voluptuousness* in which they themselves shared. For, if this happened, they found an equivalent or approximately equivalent substitute in my body for the state of heavenly bliss which they had lost, and which itself consisted in a kind of voluptuous enjoyment.' (179-80.)

Such then, was the result of the changes produced in Schreber by his illness, as we find them expressed in the two main features of his delusional system. Before it he had been inclined to sexual asceticism and had been a doubter in regard to God; while after it he was a believer in God and a devotee of voluptuousness. But just as his re-conquered belief in God was of a peculiar kind, so too the sexual enjoyment which he had won for himself was of a most unusual character. It was not the sexual liberty of a man, but the sexual feelings of a woman. He took up a feminine attitude towards God; he felt that he was God's wife.[1]

No other part of his delusions is treated by the patient so exhaustively, one might almost say so insistently, as his alleged transformation into a woman. The nerves absorbed by him have, so he says, assumed in his body the character of female nerves of voluptuousness, and have given to his body a more or less female stamp, and more particularly to his skin a softness peculiar to the female sex (87). If he presses lightly with his fingers upon any part of his body, he can feel these nerves, under the surface of the skin, as a tissue of a thread-like or stringy texture; they are especially present in the region of the chest, where, in a woman, her breasts would be. 'By applying pressure to this tissue, I am able to evoke a sensation of voluptuousness such as women experience, and especially in I think of something feminine at the same time.' (277.) He knows with certainty that this tissue was originally nothing else than nerves of God, which could hardly have lost the character of nerves merely through having passed over into his body (279). By means of what he calls 'drawing' (that is, by calling up visual images) he is able to give both himself and the rays an impression that his body is fitted out with female breasts and genitals: 'It has become so much a habit with me to draw female buttocks on to my body - *honi soit qui mal y pense* - that I do it almost involuntarily every time I stoop.' (233.) He is 'bold enough to assert that anyone who should happen to see me before the mirror with the upper portion of my torso bared

- especially if the illusion is assisted by my wearing a little
feminine finery - would receive an unmistakable impression
of a *female bust*. (280.) He calls for a medical examination,
in order to establish the fact that his whole body has nerves
of voluptuousness dispersed over it from head to foot, a
state of things which is only to be found, in his opinion,
in the female body, whereas, in the male, to the best of his
knowledge, nerves of voluptuousness exist only in the sexual
organs and their immediate vicinity (274). The spiritual
voluptuousness which has been developed owing to this
accumulation of nerves in his body is so intense that it only
requires a slight effort of his imagination (especially when
he is lying in bed) to procure him a feeling of sensual well-
being that affords a tolerably clear adumbration of the sexual
pleasure enjoyed by a woman during copulation (269).

[1] 'Something occurred in my own body similar to the conception
of Jesus Christ in an immaculate virgin, that is, in a woman
who had never had intercourse with a man. On two separate
occasions (and while I was still in Professor Flechsig's institution)
I have possessed female genitals, though somewhat imperfectly
developed ones, and have felt a stirring in my body, such as
would arise from the quickening of a human embryo. Nerves of
God corresponding to male semen had, by a divine miracle, been
projected into my body, and impregnation had thus taken place.'
(Introduction, 4.)

If we now recall the dream which the patient had during the incubation period of his illness, before he had moved to Dresden, it will become clear beyond a doubt that his delusion of being transformed into a woman was nothing else than a realization of the content of that dream. At that time he had rebelled against the dream with masculine indignation, and in the same way he began by striving against its fulfilment in his illness and looked upon his transformation into a woman as a disgrace with which he was threatened with hostile intention. But there came a time (it was in November, 1895) when he began to reconcile himself to the transformation and bring it into harmony with the higher purposes of God: 'Since then, and with a full consciousness of what I did, I have inscribed upon my banner the cultivation of femaleness.' (177-8.)

He then arrived at the firm conviction that it was God Himself who, for His own satisfaction, was demanding femaleness from him:

'No sooner, however, am I alone with God (if I may so express it), than it becomes a necessity for me to employ every imaginable device and to summon up the whole of my mental faculties, and especially my imagination, in order to bring it about that the divine rays may have the impression as continuously as possible (or, since this is beyond mortal power at least at certain times of day) that I am a woman luxuriating in voluptuous sensations.' (281.)

'On the other hand, God demands a *constant state of enjoyment*, such as would be in keeping with the conditions of existence imposed upon souls by the Order of Things; and it is my duty to provide Him with this . . . in the shape of the greatest possible generation of spiritual voluptuousness. And if, in this process, a little sensual pleasure falls to my share, I feel justified in accepting it as some slight compensation for the inordinate measure of suffering and privation that has been mine for so many past years . . .' (283.)

'. . . I think I may even venture to advance the view based upon impressions I have received, that God would never take any steps towards effecting a withdrawal - the first result of which is invariably to alter my physical condition markedly for the worse - but would quietly and permanently yield to my powers of attraction, if it were possible for me *always* to be playing the part of a woman lying in my own amorous embraces, *always* to be casting my looks upon female forms, *always* to be gazing at pictures of women, and so on.' (284-5.)

In Schreber's system the two principal elements of his delusions (his transformation into a woman and his favoured relation to God) are linked in his assumption of a feminine attitude towards God. It will be an unavoidable part of our task to show that there is an essential *genetic* relation between these two elements. Otherwise our attempts at elucidating Schreber's delusions will leave us in the absurd

position described in Kant's famous simile in the *Critique of
Pure Reason* - we shall be like a man holding a sieve under a
he-goat while some one else milks it.

II
ATTEMPTS AT INTERPRETATION

There are two angles from which we could attempt to reach an understanding of this history of a case of paranoia and to lay bare in it the familiar complexes and motive forces of mental life. We might start either from the patient's own delusional utterances or from the exciting causes of his illness.

The former method must seem enticing since the brilliant example given us by Jung in his interpretation of a case of dementia praecox which was far severer than this one and which exhibited symptoms far more remote from the normal. The high level of our present patient's intelligence, too, and his communicativeness, seem likely to facilitate the accomplishment of our task along these lines. He himself not in frequently presses the key into our hands, by adding a gloss, a quotation or an example to some delusional proposition in an apparently incidental manner, or even by expressly denying some parallel to it that has arisen in his own mind. For when this happens, we have only to follow our usual psycho-analytic technique - to strip his sentence of its negative form, to take his example as being the actual thing, or his quotation or gloss as being the original source - and we find ourselves in possession of what we are looking for, namely a translation of the paranoid mode of expression into the normal one.

It is perhaps worth giving a more detailed illustration of this procedure. Schreber complains of the nuisance created by the so-called 'miracled birds' or 'talking birds', to which he ascribes a number of very remarkable qualities (208-14). It is his belief that they are composed of former 'fore-courts of Heaven', that is, of human souls which have entered into a state of bliss, and that they have been loaded with ptomaine[1] poison and set on to him. They have been brought to the condition of repeating 'meaningless phrases which they have learnt by heart' and which have been 'dinned into them'. Each time that they have discharged their load of ptomaine poison on to him - that is each time that they have 'reeled off the phrases which have been dinned into them, as it were' - they become to some extent absorbed into his soul, with the words 'The deuce of a fellow!' or 'Deuce take it!' which are the only words they are still capable of using to express a genuine feeling. They cannot understand the meaning of the words they speak, but they are by nature susceptible to similarity of sounds, though the similarity need not necessarily be a complete one. Thus it is immaterial to them whether one says:

'*Santiago*' or '*Karthago*',
'*Chinesentum*' or '*Jesum Christum*',
'*Abendrot*' or '*Atemnot*',

'*Ariman*' or '*Ackermann*' etc.[2] (210.)

As we read this description, we cannot avoid the idea that what it really refers to must be young girls. In a carping mood people often compare them to geese, ungallantly accuse then of having 'the brains of a bird' and declare that they can say nothing but phrases learnt by rote and they betray their lack of education by confusing foreign words that sound alike. The phrase 'The deuce of a fellow!', which is the only thing that they are serious about, would in that case be an allusion to the triumph of the young man who has succeeded in impressing them. And, sure enough, a few pages later we come upon a passage in which Schreber confirms this interpretation: 'For purposes of distinction, I have as a joke given girls' names to a great number of the remaining bird-souls; since by their inquisitiveness, their voluptuous bent, etc., they one and all most readily suggest a comparison with little girls. Some of these girls' names have since been adopted by the rays of God and have been retained as a designation of the bird-souls in question.' (214.) This easy interpretation of the 'miracled birds' gives us a hint which may help us towards understanding the enigmatic 'fore-courts of Heaven'.

[1] [German '*Leichengift*', literally 'corpse poison'.]

[2] [Santiago' or 'Carthage',

'Chinese-dom' or 'Jesus Christ',

'Sunset' or 'Breathlessness',

'Ahriman' or 'Farmer'.]

I am quite aware that a psycho-analyst needs no small amount of tact and restraint whenever in the course of his work he goes beyond the typical instances of interpretation and that his listeners or readers will only follow him as far a their own familiarity with analytic technique will allow them. He has every reason, therefore, to guard against the risk that an increased display of acumen on his part may be accompanied by a diminution in the certainty and trustworthiness of his results. It is thus only natural that one analyst will tend too much in the direction of caution and another too much in the direction of boldness. It will not be possible to define the proper limits of justifiable interpretation until many experiments have been made and until the subject has become more familiar. In working upon the case of Schreber I have had a policy of restraint forced on me by the circumstance that the opposition to his publishing the *Denkwürdigkeiten* was so far effective as to withhold a considerable portion of the material from our knowledge - the portion, too, which would in all probability have thrown the most important light upon the case.[1] Thus, for instance, the third chapter of the book opens with this promising announcement: 'I shall now proceed to describe certain events which occurred to *other members of my family* and which may conceivably have been connected with the soul-murder I have postulated; for there is at any rate something more or less problematical about all of them, something not easily explicable upon the lines of ordinary human experience.' (33.) But the next sentence, which is also the last of the chapter, is as follows: 'The remainder of this chapter has been withheld from print as being unsuitable for publication.' I shall therefore have to be satisfied if I can succeed in tracing back at any rate the nucleus of the delusional structure with some degree of certainty to familiar human motives.

[1] 'When we survey the contents of this document', writes Dr. Weber in his report, 'and consider the mass of indiscretions in regard to himself and other persons which it contains, when we observe the unblushing manner in which he describes situations and events which are of the most delicate nature and indeed, in an aesthetic sense, utterly impossible, when we reflect upon his use of strong language of the most offensive kind, and so forth, we shall find it quite impossible to understand how a man, distinguished apart from this by his tact and refinement, could contemplate taking a step so compromising to himself in the public eye, unless we bear in mind the fact that . . .' etc. etc. (402.) Surely we can hardly expect that a case history which sets out to give a picture of deranged humanity and its struggles to rehabilitate itself should exhibit 'discretion' and 'aesthetic' charm.

With this object in view I shall now mention a further small piece of the case history to which sufficient weight is not given in the reports, although the patient himself has done all he can to put it in the foreground. I refer to

Schreber's relations to his first physician, Geheimrat Prof. Flechsig of Leipzig.

As we already know, Schreber's case at first took the form of delusions of persecution, and did not begin to lose it until the turning-point of his illness (the time of his 'reconciliation'). From that time onwards the persecutions became less and less intolerable, and the ignominious purpose which at first underlay his threatened emasculation began to be superseded by a purpose in consonance with the Order of Things. But the first author of all these acts of persecution was Flechsig, and he remains their instigator throughout the whole course of the illness.[1]

Of the actual nature of Flechsig's enormity and its motives the patient speaks with the characteristic vagueness and obscurity which may be regarded as marks of an especially intense work of delusion-formation, if it is legitimate to judge paranoia on the model of a far more familiar mental phenomenon - the dream. Flechsig, according to the patient, committed, or attempted to commit, 'soul-murder' upon him - an act which, he thought, was comparable with the effort made by the devil or by demons to gain possession of a soul and may have had its prototype in events which occurred between members of the Flechsig and Schreber families long since deceased (22 ff.). We should be glad to learn more of the meaning of this 'soul-murder', but at this point our sources relapse once more into a tendentious silence: 'As

to what constitutes the true essence of soul-murder, and as
to its technique, if I may so describe it, I am able to say
nothing beyond what has already been indicated. There
is only this, perhaps, to be added . . . (The passage which
follows is unsuitable for publication.)' (28.) As a result of
this omission we are left in the dark on the question of what
is meant by 'soul-murder'. We shall refer later on to the only
hint upon the subject which has evaded censorship.

[1] 'Even now the voices that talk with me call out your name
to me hundreds of times each day. They name you in certain
constantly recurring connections, and especially as being the
first author of the injuries I have suffered. And yet the personal
relations which existed between us for a time have, so far as I am
concerned, long since faded into the background; so that I myself
could have little enough reason to be for ever recalling you to my
mind, and still less for doing so with any feelings of resentment.'
('Open Letter to Professor Flechsig', viii.)

However this may be, a further development of
Schreber's delusions soon took place, which affected his
relations to God without altering his relations to Flechsig.
Hitherto he had regarded Flechsig (or rather his soul) as his
only true enemy and had looked upon God Almighty as
his ally; but now he could not avoid the thought that God
Himself had played the part of accessory, if not of instigator,
in the plot against him. (59.) Flechsig, however, remained
the first seducer, to whose influence God had yielded (60).

51

He had succeeded in making his way up to heaven with his whole soul or a part of it and in becoming a 'leader of rays', without dying or undergoing any preliminary purification.[1] (56.) The Flechsig soul continued to play this role even after the patient had been moved from the Leipzig clinic to Dr. Pierson's asylum. The influence of the new environment was shown by the Flechsig soul being joined by the soul of the chief attendant, whom the patient recognized as a person who had formerly lived in the same block of flats as himself. This was represented as being the von W. soul.[2] The Flechsig soul then introduced the system of 'soul-division', which assumed large proportions. At one time there were as many as forty to sixty sub-divisions of the Flechsig soul; two of its larger divisions were known as the 'upper Flechsig' and the 'middle Flechsig'. The von W. soul (the chief attendant's) behaved in just the same fashion (111). It was sometimes most entertaining to notice the way in which these two souls, in spite of their alliance, carried on a feud with one another, the aristocratic pride of the one pitted against the professorial vanity of the other (113). During his first weeks at Sonnenstein (to which hr, was finally moved in the summer of 1894) the soul of his new physician, Dr. Weber, came into play; and shortly afterwards the change-over took place in the development of his delusions which we have come to know as his 'reconciliation'.

¹ According to another and significant version, which, however, was soon rejected, Professor Flechsig had shot himself either at Weissenburg in Alsace or in a police cell at Leipzig. The patient saw his funeral go past, though not in the direction that was to be expected in view of the relative positions of the University Clinic and the cemetery. On other occasions Flechsig appeared to him in the company of a policeman, or in conversation with his wife. Schreber was a witness of this conversation by the method of 'nerve-connection', and in the course of it Professor Flechsig called himself 'God Flechsig' to his wife, so that she was inclined to think he had gone mad. (82.)

² The voices informed him that in the course of an official enquiry this von W. had made some untrue statements about him, either deliberately or out of carelessness, and in particular had accused him of masturbation. As a punishment for this he was now obliged to wait on the patient (108).

During this later stay at Sonnenstein, when God had begun to appreciate him better, a raid was made upon the souls, which had been multiplied so much as to become a nuisance. As a result of this, the Flechsig soul survived in only one or two shapes, and the von W. soul in only a single one. The latter soon disappeared altogether. The divisions of the Flechsig soul, which slowly lost both their intelligence and their power, then came to be described as the 'posterior Flechsig' and the '"Oh well!" Party'. That the Flechsig soul retained its importance to the last, is made clear by

Schreber's prefatory 'Open Letter to Herr Geheimrat Prof.
Dr. Flechsig'.

In this remarkable document Schreber expresses his
firm conviction that the physician who influenced him had
the same visions and received the same disclosures upon
supernatural things as he himself. He protests on the very
first page that the author of the *Denkwürdigkeiten* has not
the remotest intention of making an attack upon the doctor's
honour, and the same point is earnestly and emphatically
repeated in the patient's presentations of his position (343,
445). It is evident that he is endeavouring to distinguish the
'soul Flechsig' from the living man of the same name, the
Flechsig of his delusions from the real Flechsig.[1]

[1] 'I am accordingly obliged *to admit as a possibility* that
everything in the first chapters of my *Denkwürdigkeiten* which
is connected with the name of Flechsig may only refer to the
soul Flechsig as distinguished from the living man. For that his
soul has a separate existence is a certain fact, though it cannot be
explained upon any natural basis.' (342-3.)

The study of a number of cases of delusions of persecution
has led me as well as other investigators to the view that
the relation between the patient and his persecutor can be
reduced to a simple formula.[1] It appears that the person to
whom the delusion ascribes so much power and influence,
in whose hands all the threads of the conspiracy converge, is,
if he is definitely named, either identical with some one who

played an equally important part in the patient's emotional life before his illness, or is easily recognizable as a substitute for him. The intensity of the emotion is projected in the shape of external power, while its quality is changed into the opposite. The person who is now hated and feared for being a persecutor was at one time loved and honoured. The main purpose of the persecution asserted by the patient's delusion is to justify the change in his emotional attitude.

Bearing this point of view in mind, let us now examine the relations which had formerly existed between Schreber and his physician and persecutor, Flechsig. We have already heard that, in the years 1884 and 1885, Schreber suffered from a first attack of nervous disorder, which ran its course 'without the occurrence of any incidents bordering upon the sphere of the supernatural' (35). While he was in this condition, which was described as 'hypochondria' and seems not to have overstepped the limits of a neurosis, Flechsig acted as his doctor. At that time Schreber spent six months in the University Clinic at Leipzig. We learn that after his recovery he had cordial feelings towards his doctor. 'The main thing was that, after a fairly long period of convalescence which I spent in travelling, I was finally cured; and it was therefore impossible that I should feel anything at that time but the liveliest gratitude towards Professor Flechsig. I gave a marked expression to this feeling both in a personal visit which I subsequently paid him and in what I deemed to be an appropriate honorarium.' (35-6.) It is true that Schreber's encomium in the *Denkwürdigkeiten* upon this first treatment of Flechsig's is not entirely with out reservations; but that can easily be understood if we consider that his attitude had in the meantime been reversed. The passage immediately following the one that has just been quoted bears witness to the original warmth of his feelings towards the physician who had treated him so successfully: 'The gratitude of my wife was perhaps even more heartfelt; for she revered Professor Flechsig as the man who had restored her husband to her, and hence it was that for years she kept his portrait standing upon her writing-table.' (36.)

[1] Cf. Abraham, 1908. In the course of this paper its author, referring to a correspondence between us, scrupulously attributes to myself an influence upon the development of his views.

Since we cannot obtain any insight into the causes of the first illness (a knowledge of which is undoubtedly indispensable for properly elucidating the second and severer illness) we must now plunge at random into an unknown concatenation of circumstances. During the incubation period of his illness, as we are aware (that is, between June 1893, when he was appointed to his new post, and the following October, when he took up his duties), he repeatedly dreamt that his old nervous disorder had returned. Once, moreover, when he was half asleep, he had a feeling that after all it must be nice to be a woman submitting to the act of copulation.

The dreams and the phantasy are reported by Schreber in immediate succession; and if we also bring together their subject-matter, we shall be able to infer that, at the same time as his recollection of his illness, a recollection of his doctor was also aroused in his mind, and that the feminine attitude which he assumed in the phantasy was from the first directed towards the doctor. Or it may be that the dream of his illness having returned simply expressed some such longing as: 'I wish I could see Flechsig again!' Our ignorance of the mental content of the first illness bars our way in this direction. Perhaps that illness had left behind in him a feeling of affectionate dependence upon his doctor, which had now, for some unknown reason, become intensified to the pitch of an erotic desire. This feminine phantasy which was still kept impersonal, was met at once by an indignant repudiation - a true 'masculine protest', to use Adler's expression, but in a sense different from his.[1] But in the severe psychosis which broke out soon afterwards the feminine phantasy carried everything before it; and it only requires a slight correction of the characteristic paranoic indefiniteness of Schreber's mode of expression to enable us to divine the fact that the patient was in fear of sexual abuse at the hands of his doctor himself. The exciting cause of his illness, then, was an outburst of homosexual libido; the object of this libido was probably from the very first his doctor, Flechsig; and his struggles against the libidinal impulse produced the conflict which gave rise to the symptoms.

[1] Adler (1910). According to Adler the masculine protest has a share in the production of the symptom, whereas in the present instance the patient is protesting against a symptom that is already fully fledged.

I will pause here for a moment to meet a storm of remonstrances and objections. Any one acquainted with the present state of psychiatry must be prepared to face trouble.

'Is it not an act of irresponsible levity, an indiscretion and a calumny, to charge a man of such high ethical standing as the former Senatspräsident Schreber with homosexuality?' - No. The patient has himself informed the world at large of his phantasy of being transformed into a woman, and he has allowed all personal considerations to be outweighed by interests of a higher nature. Thus he has himself given us the right to occupy ourselves with his phantasy, and in translating it into the technical terminology of medicine we have not made the slightest addition to its content.

'Yes, but he was not in his right mind when he did it. His delusion that he was being transformed into a woman was a pathological idea.' - We have not forgotten that. Indeed our only concern is with the meaning and origin of this pathological idea. We will appeal to the distinction he himself draws between the man Flechsig and the 'Flechsig soul'. We are not making reproaches of any kind against him

- whether for having had homosexual impulses or for having endeavoured to suppress them. Psychiatrists should at last take a lesson from this patient, when they see him trying, in spite of his delusions, not to confuse the world of the unconscious with the world of reality.

'But it is nowhere expressly stated that the transformation into a woman which he so much dreaded was to be carried out for the benefit of Flechsig.' - That is true; and it is not difficult to understand why, in preparing his memoirs for publication, since he was anxious not to insult the 'man Flechsig', he should have avoided so gross an accusation. But the toning-down of his language owing to these considerations did not go so far as to be able to conceal the true meaning of his accusation. Indeed, it may be maintained that after all it is expressed openly in such a passage as the following: 'In this way a conspiracy against me was brought to a head (in about March or April, 1894). Its object was to contrive that, when once my nervous complaint had been recognized as incurable or assumed to be so, *I should be handed over to a certain person* in such a manner that my soul should be delivered up to him, but my body . . . should be transformed into a female body, and *as such surrendered to the person in question* with a view to sexual abuse . . .'[1] (56). It is unnecessary to remark that no other individual is ever named who could be put in Flechsig's place. Towards the end of Schreber's stay in the clinic at Leipzig, a fear occurred to his mind that he 'was to be thrown to the attendants' for the purpose of sexual abuse (98). Any remaining doubts that we have upon the nature of the part originally attributed to the doctor are dispelled when, in the later stages of his delusion, we find Schreber outspokenly admitting his feminine attitude towards God. The other accusation against Flechsig echoes over-loudly through the book. Flechsig, he says, tried to commit soul-murder upon him. As we already know, the patient was himself not clear as to the actual nature of that crime, but it was connected with matters of discretion which precluded their publication (as we see from the suppressed third chapter). From this point a single thread takes us further. Schreber illustrates the nature of soul-murder by referring to the legends embodied in Goethe's *Faust*, Byron's *Manfred*, Weber's *Freischütz*, etc. (22), and one of these instances is further cited in another passage. In discussing the division of God into two persons, Schreber identifies his 'lower God' and 'upper God' with Ahriman and Ormuzd respectively (19); and a little later a casual footnote occurs: 'Moreover, the name of Ahriman also appears in connection with a soul-murder in, for example, Lord Byron's *Manfred*.' (20.) In the play which is thus referred to there is scarcely anything comparable to the bartering of Faust's soul, and I have searched it in vain for the expression 'soul-murder'. But the essence and the secret of the whole work lies in - an incestuous relation between a brother and a sister. And here our thread breaks off short.[2]

[1] The italics in this passage are mine.

[2] By way of substantiating the above assertion I will quote a passage from the last scene of the play, in which Manfred says to the demon who has come to fetch him away:

. . . my past power
Was purchased by no compact with thy crew.

There is thus a direct contradiction of a soul having been bartered. This mistake on Schreber's part was probably not without its significance. - It is plausible, by the way, to connect the plot of *Manfred* with the incestuous relations which have repeatedly been asserted to exist between the poet and his half-sister. And it is not a little striking that the action of Byron's other play, his celebrated *Cain*, should be laid in the primal family, where no objections could exist to incest between brother and sister. - Finally, we cannot leave the subject of soul-murder without quoting one more passage from the *Denkwürdigkeiten*: 'in this connection Flechsig used formerly to be named as the first author of soul-murder, whereas for some time past the facts have been deliberately inverted and an attempt has been made to "represent" myself as being the one who practises soul-murder . . .' (23.)

At a later stage in this paper I intend to return to a discussion of some further objections; but in the meantime I shall consider myself justified in maintaining the view that the basis of Schreber's illness was the outburst of a homosexual impulse. This hypothesis harmonizes with a noteworthy detail of the case history, which remains otherwise inexplicable. The patient had a fresh 'nervous collapse', which exercised a decisive effect upon the course of his illness, at a time when his wife was taking a short holiday on account of her own health. Up till then she had spent several hours with him every day and had taken her mid-day meal with him. But when she returned after an absence of four days, she found him most sadly altered: so much so, indeed, that he himself no longer wished to see her. 'What especially determined my mental break-down was a particular night, during which I had a quite extraordinary number of emissions - quite half a dozen, all in that one night.' (44.) It is easy to understand that the mere presence of his wife must have acted as a protection against the attractive power of the men about him; and if we are prepared to admit that an emission cannot occur in an adult without some mental concomitant, we shall be able to supplement the patient's emissions that night by assuming that they were accompanied by homosexual phantasies which remained unconscious.

The question of why this outburst of homosexual libido overtook the patient precisely at this period (that is, between the dates of his appointment and of his move to Dresden) cannot be answered in the absence of more precise knowledge of the story of his life. Generally speaking, every human being oscillates all through his life between heterosexual and homosexual feelings, and any frustration or disappointment in the one direction is apt to drive him over into the other. We know nothing of these factors in Schreber's case, but we must not omit to draw attention to a somatic factor which may very well have been relevant. At the time of this illness Dr. Schreber was fifty-one years old, and he had therefore reached an age which is of critical importance in sexual life. It is a period at which in women the sexual function, after a phase of intensified activity, enters upon a process of far-reaching involution; nor do men appear to be exempt from its influence, for men as well as women are subject to a 'climacteric' and to the susceptibilities to disease which go along with it.[1]

[1] I owe my knowledge of Schreber's age at the time of his illness to some information which was kindly given me by one of his relatives, through the agency of Dr. Stegmann of Dresden. Apart from this one fact, however, I have made use of no material in this paper that is not derived from the actual text of the *Denkwürdigkeiten.*

I can well imagine what a dubious hypothesis it must appear to be to suppose that a man's friendly feeling towards his doctor can suddenly break out in an intensified form after a lapse of eight years[1] and become the occasion of such a severe mental disorder. But I do not think we should be justified in dismissing such a hypothesis merely on account of its inherent improbability, if it recommends itself to us on other grounds; we ought rather to inquire how far we shall get if we follow it up. For the improbability may be of a passing kind and may be due to the fact that the doubtful hypothesis has not as yet been brought into relation with any other pieces of knowledge and that it is the first hypothesis with which the problem has been approached. But for the benefit of those who are unable to hold their judgement in suspense and who regard our hypothesis as altogether untenable, it is easy to suggest a possibility which would rob it of its bewildering character. The patient's friendly feeling towards his doctor may very well have been due to a process of 'transference', by means of which an emotional cathexis became transposed from some person who was important to him on to the doctor who was in reality indifferent to him; so that the doctor will have been chosen as a deputy or surrogate for some one much closer to him. To put the matter in a more concrete form: the patient was reminded of his brother or father by the figure of the doctor, he rediscovered them in him; there will then be nothing to wonder at if, in certain circumstances, a longing for the surrogate figure reappeared in him and operated with a violence that is only to be explained in the light of its origin and primary significance.

With a view to following up this attempt at an explanation, I naturally thought it worth while discovering whether the patient's father was still alive at the time at which he fell ill, whether he had had a brother, and if so whether he was then living or among the 'blest'. I was pleased, therefore, when, after a prolonged search through the pages of the *Denkwürdigkeiten*, I came at last upon a passage in which the patient sets these doubts at rest: 'The memory of my father and my brother . . . is as sacred to me as . . .' etc. (442.) So that both of them were dead at the time of the onset of his second illness (and, it may be, of his first illness as well).

We shall therefore, I think, raise no further objections to the hypothesis that the exciting cause of the illness was the appearance in him of a feminine (that is, a passive homosexual) wishful phantasy, which took as its object the figure of his doctor. An intense resistance to this phantasy arose on the part of Schreber's personality, and the ensuing defensive struggle, which might perhaps just as well have assumed some other shape, took on, for reasons unknown to us, that of a delusion of persecution. The person he longed for now became his persecutor, and the content of his wishful phantasy became the content of his persecution. It may be presumed that the same schematic outline will turn out to be applicable to other cases of delusions of persecution. What distinguishes Schreber's case from others, however, is its

further development and the transformation it underwent
in the course of it.

¹ This was the length of the interval between Schreber's first and
second illnesses.

One such change was the replacement of Flechsig by
the superior figure of God. This seems at first as though it
were a sign of aggravation of the conflict, an intensification
of the unbearable persecution, but it soon becomes evident
that it was preparing the way for the second change and, with
it, the solution of the conflict. It was impossible for Schreber
to become reconciled to playing the part of a female wanton
towards his doctor; but the task of providing God Himself
with the voluptuous sensations that He required called up
no such resistance on the part of his ego. Emasculation was
now no longer a disgrace; it became 'consonant with the
Order of Things', it took its place in a great cosmic chain of
events, and was instrumental in the re-creation of humanity
after its extinction. 'A new race of men, born from the spirit
of Schreber' would, so he thought, revere as their ancestor
this man who believed himself the victim of persecution. By
this means an outlet was provided which would satisfy both
of the contending forces. His ego found compensation in his
megalomania, while his feminine wishful phantasy made its
way through and became acceptable. The struggle and the
illness could cease. The patient's sense of reality, however,
which had in the meantime become stronger, compelled

him to postpone the solution from the present to the remote
future, and to content himself with what might be described
as an asymptotic wish-fulfilment.[1] Some time or other, he
anticipated, his transformation into a woman would come
about; until then the personality of Dr. Schreber would
remain indestructible.

In textbooks of psychiatry we frequently come across
statements to the effect that megalomania can develop out
of delusions of persecution. The process is supposed to be
as follows. The patient is primarily the victim of a delusion
that he is being persecuted by powers of the greatest might.
He then feels a need to account to himself for this, and in
that way hits on the idea that he himself is a very exalted
personage and worthy of such persecution. The development
of megalomania is thus attributed by the textbooks to a
process which (borrowing a useful word from Ernest Jones)
we may describe as 'rationalization'. But to ascribe such
important affective consequences to a rationalization is, as
it seems to us, an entirely unpsychological proceeding; and
we would consequently draw a sharp distinction between
our opinion and the one which we have quoted from the
textbooks. We are making no claim, for the moment, to
knowing the origin of the megalomania.

[1] 'It is only, he writes towards the end of the book, 'as
possibilities which must be taken into account, that I mention
that my emasculation may even yet be accomplished and may

result in a new generation issuing from my womb by divine impregnation.' (293.)

Turning once more to the case of Schreber, we are bound to admit that any attempt at throwing light upon the transformation in his delusion brings us up against extraordinary difficulties. In what manner and by what means was the ascent from Flechsig to God brought about? From what source did he derive the megalomania which so fortunately enabled him to become reconciled to his persecution, or, in analytical phraseology, to accept the wishful phantasy which had had to be repressed? The *Denkwürdigkeiten* give us a first clue; for they show us that in the patient's mind 'Flechsig' and 'God' belonged to the same class. In one of his phantasies he overheard a conversation between Flechsig and his wife, in which the former asserted that he was 'God Flechsig', so that his wife thought he had gone mad (82). But there is another feature in the development of Schreber's delusions which claims our attention. If we take a survey of the delusions as a whole we see that the persecutor is divided into Flechsig and God; in just the same way Flechsig himself subsequently splits up into two personalities, the 'upper' and the 'middle' Flechsig, and God into the 'lower' and the 'upper' God. In the later stages of the illness the decomposition of Flechsig goes further still (193). A process of decomposition of this kind is very characteristic of paranoia. Paranoia decomposes just as hysteria condenses.

Or rather, paranoia resolves once more into their elements the products of the condensations and identifications which are effected in the unconscious. The frequent repetition of the decomposing process in Schreber's case would, according to Jung, be an expression of the importance which the person in question possessed for him.[1] All of this dividing up of Flechsig and God into a number of persons thus had the same meaning as the splitting of the persecutor into Flechsig and God. They were all duplications of one and the same important relationship.[2] But, in order to interpret all these details, we must further draw attention to our view of this decomposition of the persecutor into Flechsig and God as a paranoid reaction to a previously established identification of the two figures or their belonging to the same class. If the persecutor Flechsig was originally a person whom Schreber loved, then God must also simply be the reappearance of some one else whom he loved, and probably some one of greater importance.

[1] Jung (1910*a*). Jung is probably right when he goes on to say that the decomposition follows the general lines taken by schizophrenia in that it uses a process of analysis in order to produce a watering-down effect, and is thus designed to prevent the occurrence of unduly powerful impressions. When, however, one of his patients said to him: 'Oh, are you Dr. J. too? There was some one here this morning who said he was Dr. J.', we must interpret it as being an admission to this effect: 'You remind me

now of a different member of the class of my transferences from
the one you reminded me of when you visited me last.'

[2] Otto Rank (1909) has found the same process at work in the
formation of myths.

If we pursue this train of thought, which seems to be
a legitimate one, we shall be driven to the conclusion that
the other person must have been his father; this makes it all
the clearer that Flechsig must have stood for his brother -
who, let us hope, may have been older than himself.[1] The
feminine phantasy, which aroused such violent opposition in
the patient, thus had its root in a longing, intensified to an
erotic pitch, for his father and brother. This feeling, so far as
it referred to his brother, passed, by a process of transference,
on to his doctor, Flechsig; and when it was carried back on
to his father a settlement of the conflict was reached.

We shall not feel that we have been justified in thus
introducing Schreber's father into his delusions, unless the
new hypothesis shows itself of some use to us in understanding
the case and in elucidating details of the delusions which are
as yet unintelligible. It will be recalled that Schreber's God
and his relations to Him exhibited the most curious features:
how they showed the strangest mixture of blasphemous
criticism and mutinous insubordination on the one hand
and of reverent devotion on the other. God, according to
him, had succumbed to the misleading influence of Flechsig:
He was incapable of learning anything by experience, and

did not understand living men because He only knew how to deal with corpses; and He manifested His power in a succession of miracles which, striking though they might be, were none the less futile and silly.

[1] No information on this point is to be found in the *Denkwürdigkeiten*.

Now the father of Senatspräsident Dr. Schreber was no insignificant person. He was the Dr. Daniel Gottlob Moritz Schreber whose memory is kept green to this day by the numerous Schreber Associations which flourish especially in Saxony; and, moreover, he was a *physician*. His activities in favour of promoting the harmonious upbringing of the young, of securing co-ordination between education in the home and in the school, of introducing physical culture and manual work with a view to raising the standards of health - all this exerted a lasting influence upon his contemporaries.[1] His great reputation as the founder of therapeutic gymnastics in Germany is still shown by the wide circulation of his *Ärtzliche Zimmergymnastik* in medical circles and the numerous editions through which it has passed.

Such a father as this was by no means unsuitable for transfiguration into a God in the affectionate memory of the son from whom he had been so early separated by death. It is true that we cannot help feeling that there is an impassable gulf between the personality of God and that of any human being, however eminent he may be. But we must ber that this has not always been so. The gods of the peoples of antiquity stood in a closer human relationship to them. The Romans used to deify their dead emperors as a matter of routine; and the Emperor Vespasian, a sensible and competent man, exclaimed when he was first taken ill: 'Alas! Methinks I am becoming a God!'[2]

[1] I have to thank my colleague Dr. Stegmann of Dresden for his kindness in letting me see a copy of a journal entitled *Der Freund der Schreber-Vereine* [*The Friend of the Schreber Associations*]. This number (Vol. II. No. 10) celebrates the centenary of Dr. Schreber's birth, and some biographical data are contained in it. Dr. Schreber senior was born in 1808 and died in 1861, at the age of only fifty-three. From the source which I have already mentioned I know that our patient was at that time nineteen years old.

[2] Suetonius, *Lives of the Caesars*, Book VIII, Chapter 23. This practice of deification began with Julius Caesar. Augustus styled himself '*Divi filius*' ['the son of the God'] in his inscriptions.

We are perfectly familiar with the infantile attitude of boys towards their father; it is composed of the same mixture of reverent submission and mutinous insubordination that we have found in Schreber's relation to his God, and is the unmistakable prototype of that relation, which is faithfully copied from it. But the circumstance that Schreber's father was a physician, and a most eminent physician, and one who was no doubt highly respected by his patients, is what

explains the most striking characteristics of his God and
those upon which he dwells in such a critical fashion. Could
more bitter scorn be shown for such a physician than by
declaring that he understands nothing about living men
and only knows how to deal with corpses? No doubt it is
an essential attribute of God to perform miracles; but a
physician performs miracles too; he effects miraculous cures,
as his enthusiastic clients proclaim. So that when we see that
these very miracles (the material for which was provided by
the patient's hypochondria) turn out to be incredible, absurd,
and to some extent positively silly, we are reminded of the
assertion in my *Interpretation of Dreams* that absurdity in
dreams expresses ridicule and derision.[1] Evidently, therefore,
it is used for the same purposes in paranoia. As regards some
of the other reproaches which he levelled against God, such,
for instance, as that He learned nothing by experience, it is
natural to suppose that they are examples of the *tu quoque*
mechanism used by children,[2] which, when they receive
a reproof, flings it back unchanged upon the person who
originated it. Similarly, the voices give us grounds for
suspecting that the accusation of soul-murder brought
against Flechsig was in the first instance a self-accusation.[3]

[1] p. 891.

[2] It looks remarkably like a *revanche* of this sort when we find the
patient writing out the following memorandum one day: 'Any

*attempt at exercising an educative influence must be abandoned as
hopeless.'* (188.) The uneducable one was God.

[3] 'Whereas for some time past the facts have been deliberately
inverted and an attempt has been made to "represent" myself as
being the one who practises soul-murder . . .' etc. (23).

Emboldened by the discovery that his father's profession
helps to explain the peculiarities of Schreber's God, we shall
now venture upon an interpretation which may throw some
light upon the remarkable structure of that Being. The
heavenly world consisted, as we know, of the 'anterior realms
of God' which were also called the 'fore-courts of Heaven'
and which contained the souls of the dead, and of the 'lower'
and the 'upper' God, who together constituted the 'posterior
realms of God' (19). Although we must be prepared to find
that there is a condensation here which we shall not be able
to resolve, it is nevertheless worth while referring to a clue
that is already in our hands. If the 'miracled' birds, which
have been shown to be girls, were originally fore-courts of
Heaven, may it not be that the *anterior* realms of God and
the fore-courts[1] of Heaven are to be regarded as a symbol of
what is female, and the *posterior* realms of God as a symbol
of what is male? If we knew for certain that Schreber's dead
brother was older than himself, we might suppose that the
decomposition of God into the lower and the upper God
gave expression to the patient's recollection that after his

74

father's early death his elder brother had stepped into his place.

In this connection, finally, I should like to draw attention to the subject of the *sun*, which, through its 'rays', came to have so much importance in the expression of his delusions. Schreber has a quite peculiar relation to the sun. It speaks to him in human language, and thus reveals itself to him as a living being, or as the organ of a yet higher being lying behind it (9). We learn from a medical report that at one time he 'used to shout threats and abuse at it and positively bellow at it' (382)[2] and used to call out to it that it must crawl away from him and hide. He himself tells us that the sun turns pale before him.[3] The manner in which it is bound up with his fate is shown by the important alterations it undergoes as soon as changes begin to occur in him, as, for instance, during his first weeks at Sonnenstein (135). Schreber makes it easy for us to interpret this solar myth of his. He identifies the sun directly with God, sometimes with the lower God (Ahriman),4 and sometimes with the upper. 'On the following day . . . I saw the upper God (Ormuzd), and this time not with my spiritual eyes but with my bodily ones. It was the sun, but not the sun in its ordinary aspect, as it is known to all men; it was . . .' etc. (137-8.) It is therefore no more than consistent of him to treat it in the same way as he treats God Himself.

he German word '*Vorhof*' besides having the literal meaning
ᴜᵢ ᵢore-court', is used in anatomy as a synonym for the

'vestibulum', a region of the female genitals.]

[2] 'The sun is a whore', he used to exclaim (384).

[3] 'To some extent, moreover, even to this day the sun presents a different picture to my eyes from what it did before my illness. When I stand facing it and speak aloud, its rays turn pale before me. I can gaze at it without any difficulty and without being more than slightly dazzled by it; whereas in my healthy days it would have been as impossible for me as for anyone else to gaze at it for a minute at a time.' (139, footnote.)

4 'Since July, 1894, the voices that talk to me have identified him directly with the sun.' (88.)

The sun, therefore, is nothing but another sublimated symbol for the father; and in pointing this out I must disclaim all responsibility for the monotony of the solutions provided by psycho-analysis. In this instance symbolism overrides grammatical gender - at least so far as German goes,[1] for in most other languages the sun is masculine. Its counterpart in this picture of the two parents is 'Mother Earth' as she is generally called. We frequently come upon confirmations of this assertion in resolving the pathogenic phantasies of neurotics by psycho-analysis. I can make no more than the barest allusion to the relation of all this to cosmic myths. One of my patients, who had lost his father at a very early age, was always seeking to rediscover him in what was grand and sublime in Nature. Since I have known this, it has seemed to me probable that Nietzsche's hymn 'Vor Sonnenaufgang' ['Before Sunrise'] is an expression of the same longing.[2] Another patient, who became neurotic after his father's death, was seized with his first attack of anxiety and giddiness while the sun shone upon him as he was working in the garden with a spade. He spontaneously put forward as an interpretation that he had become frightened because his father had looked at him while he was at work upon his mother with a sharp instrument. When I ventured upon a mild remonstrance, he gave an air of greater plausibility to his view by telling me that even in his father's lifetime he had compared him with the sun, though then it had been in a satirical sense. Whenever he had been asked where his father was going to spend the summer he had replied in these sonorous words from the 'Prologue in Heaven':

Und seine vorgeschrieb'ne Reise

Vollendet er mit Donnergang.[3]

His father, acting on medical advice, had been in the habit of paying an annual visit to Marienbad. This patient's infantile attitude towards his father took effect in two successive phases. As long as his father was alive it showed itself in unmitigated rebelliousness and open discord, but immediately after his death it took the form of a neurosis based upon abject submission and deferred obedience to him.

¹ [The German word for 'sun' is feminine: '

die Sonne'.]

² *Also Sprach Zarathustra*, Part III. It was only as a child that Nietzsche too knew his father.

³ ['And with a tread of thunder he accomplishes his prescribed journey.']

Thus in the case of Schreber we find ourselves once again on the familiar ground of the father-complex.¹ The patient's struggle with Flechsig became revealed to him as a conflict with God, and we must therefore construe it as an infantile conflict with the father whom he loved; the details of that conflict (of which we know nothing) are what determined the content of his delusions. None of the material which in other cases of the sort is brought to light by analysis is absent in the present one: every element is hinted at in one way or another. In infantile experiences such as this the father appears as an interferer with the satisfaction which the child is trying to obtain; this is usually of an auto-erotic character, though at a later date it is often replaced in phantasy by some other satisfaction of a less inglorious kind.² In the final stage of Schreber's delusion a magnificent victory was scored by the infantile sexual urge; for voluptuousness became God-fearing, and God Himself (his father) never tired of demanding it from him. His father's most dreaded threat, castration, actually provided the material for his wishful phantasy (at first resisted but later accepted) of being transformed into a woman. His allusion to an offence covered by the surrogate idea 'soul-murder' could not be more transparent. The chief attendant was discovered to be identical with his neighbour von W., who, according to the voices, had falsely accused him of masturbation (108). The voices said, as though giving grounds for the threat of castration: 'For you are to be *represented* as being given over to voluptuous excesses.'[3] (127-8.) Finally, we come to the enforced thinking (47) to which the patient submitted himself because he supposed that God would believe he had become an idiot and would withdraw from him if he ceased thinking for a moment. This is a reaction (with which we are also familiar in other connections) to the threat or fear of losing one's reason[4] as a result of indulging in sexual practices and especially in masturbation. Considering the enormous number of delusional ideas of a hypochondriacal nature[5] which the patient developed, no great importance should perhaps be attached to the fact that some of them coincide word for word with the hypochondriacal fears of masturbators.[6]

[1] In the same way, Schreber's 'feminine wishful phantasy' is simply one of the typical forms taken by the infantile nuclear complex.

2 See some remarks on this subject in my analysis of the 'Rat Man'.

3 The systems of 'representing' and of 'noting down' (126), taken in conjunction with the 'proved souls', point back to experiences in the patient's school days.

4 'This was the end in view, as was frankly admitted at an earlier date in the phrase "We want to destroy your reason", which I have heard proceeding from the upper God upon countless occasions.' (206 *n.*)

5 I must not omit to remark at this point that I shall not consider any theory of paranoia trustworthy unless it also covers the *hypochondriacal* symptoms by which that disorder is almost invariably accompanied. It seems to me that hypochondria stands in the same relation to paranoia as anxiety neurosis does to hysteria.

6 'For this reason attempts were made to pump out my spinal cord. This was done by means of so-called "little men" who were placed in my feet. I shall have more to say presently on the subject of these "little men", who showed some resemblance to the phenomena of the same name which I have already discussed in Chapter VI. There used as a rule to be two of them - a "little Flechsig" and a "little von W." - And I used to hear their voices, too, in my feet.' (154.) Von W. was the man who was supposed to have accused Schreber of masturbation. The 'little men' are described by Schreber himself as being among the most remarkable and, in some respects, the most puzzling phenomena

80

of his illness (157). It looks as though they were the product of a condensation of children and - spermatozoa.

Any one who was more daring than I am in making interpretations, or who was in touch with Schreber's family and consequently better acquainted with the society in which he moved and the small events of his life, would find it an easy matter to trace back innumerable details of his delusions to their sources and so discover their meaning, and this in spite of the censorship to which the *Denkwürdigkeiten* have been subjected. But as it is, we must necessarily content ourselves with this shadowy sketch of the infantile material which was used by the paranoic disorder in portraying the current conflict.

Perhaps I may be allowed to add a few words with a view to establishing the causes of this conflict that broke out it relation to the feminine wishful phantasy. As we know, when a wishful phantasy makes its appearance, our business is to bring it into connection with some *frustration*, some privation in real life. Now Schreber admits having suffered a privation of the kind. His marriage, which he describes as being in other respects a happy one, brought him no children; and in particular it brought him no son who might have consoled him for the loss of his father and brother and upon whom he might have drained off his unsatisfied homosexual affections.[1] His family line threatened to die out, and it seems that he felt no little pride in his birth and

e. 'Both the Flechsigs and the Schrebers were members of "the highest nobility of Heaven", as the phrase went. The Schrebers in particular bore the title of "Margraves of Tuscany and Tasmania"; for souls, urged by some sort of personal vanity, have a custom of adorning themselves with somewhat high-sounding titles borrowed from this world.'[2] (24.) The great Napoleon obtained a divorce from Josephine (though only after severe internal struggles) because she could not propagate the dynasty.[3] Dr. Schreber may have formed a phantasy that if he were a woman he would manage the business of having children more successfully; and he may thus have found his way back into the feminine attitude towards his father which he had exhibited in the earliest years of his childhood. If that were so, then his delusion that as a result of his emasculation the world was to be peopled with 'a new race of men, born from the spirit of Schreber' (288) - a delusion the realization of which he was continually postponing to a more and more remote future - would also be designed to offer him an escape from his childlessness. If the 'little men' whom Schreber himself finds so puzzling were children, then we should have no difficulty in understanding why they were collected in such great numbers on his head (158): they were in truth the 'children of his spirit'.[4]

[1] 'After my recovery from my first illness I spent eight years with my wife - years, upon the whole, of great happiness, rich in outward honours, and only clouded from time to time by

the oft-repeated disappointment of our hope that we might be blessed with children.' (36).

[2] He goes on from this remark, which preserves in his delusions the good-natured irony of his saner days, to trace back through former centuries the relations between the Flechsig and Schreber families. In just the same way a young man who is newly engaged, and cannot understand how he can have lived so many years without knowing the girl he is now in love with, will insist that he really made her acquaintance at some earlier time.

[3] In this connection it is worth mentioning a protest entered by the patient against some statements made in the medical report: 'I have never trifled with the idea of obtaining a *divorce*, nor have I displayed any indifference to the maintenance of our marriage tie, such as might be inferred from the expression used in the report to the effect that "I am always ready with the rejoinder that my wife can get a divorce if she likes".' (436.)

[4] Cf. what I have said about the method of representing patrilineal descent and about the birth of Athena in my analysis of the 'Rat Man' (1909*d*), p. 2183 *n*.

III
ON THE MECHANISM OF PARANOIA

We have hitherto been dealing with the father-complex, which was the dominant element in Schreber's case and with the wishful phantasy round which the illness centred. But in all of this there is nothing characteristic of the form of disease known as paranoia, nothing that might not be found (and that has not in fact been found) in other kinds of neuroses. The distinctive character of paranoia (or of dementia paranoides) must be sought for elsewhere - namely, in the particular form assumed by the symptoms; and we shall expect to find that this is determined, not by the nature of the complexes themselves, but by the mechanism by which the symptoms are formed or by which repression is brought about. We should be inclined to say that what was characteristically paranoic about the illness was the fact that the patient, as a means of warding off a homosexual wishful phantasy, reacted precisely with delusions of persecution of this kind.

These considerations therefore lend an added weight to the circumstance that we are in point of fact driven by experience to attribute to homosexual wishful phantasies an intimate (perhaps an invariable) relation to this particular form of disease. Distrusting my own experience on the subject, I have during the last few years joined with my friends C. G. Jung of Zurich and Sándor Ferenczi of Budapest in investigating upon this single point a number of cases of paranoid disorder which have come under observation. The patients whose histories provided the material for this enquiry included both men and women, and varied in race, occupation, and social standing. Yet we were astonished to find that in all of these cases defence against a homosexual wish was clearly recognizable at the very centre of the conflict which underlay the disease and that it was in an attempt to master an unconsciously reinforced current of homosexuality that they had all of them come to grief.[1] This was certainly not what we had expected. Paranoia is precisely a disorder in which a sexual aetiology is by no means obvious; far from this, the strikingly prominent features in the causation of paranoia, especially among males, are social humiliations and slights. But if we go into the matter only a little more deeply, we shall be able to see that the really operative factor in these social injuries lies in the part played in them by the homosexual components of emotional life. So long as the individual is functioning normally and it is consequently impossible to see into the depths of his mental life, we may doubt whether his emotional relations to his neighbours in society have anything to do with sexuality, either actually or in their genesis. But delusions never fail to uncover these relations and to trace back the social feelings to their roots

in a directly sensual erotic wish. So long as he was healthy,
Dr. Schreber, too, whose delusions culminated in a wishful
phantasy of an unmistakably homosexual nature, had, by all
accounts, shown no signs of homosexuality in the ordinary
sense of the word.

¹ Further confirmation is afforded by Maeder's analysis of a
paranoid patient J. B. (1910). The present paper, I regret to say,
was completed before I had an opportunity of reading Maeder's
work.

I shall now endeavour (and I think the attempt is neither
unnecessary nor unjustifiable) to show that the knowledge
of psychological processes, which, thanks to psycho-analysis,
we now possess, already enables us to understand the part
played by a homosexual wish in the development of paranoia.
Recent investigations¹ have directed our attention to a stage
in the development of the libido which it passes through on
the way from auto-erotism to object-love.² This stage has
been given the name of narcissism. What happens is this.
There comes a time in the development of the individual at
which he unifies his sexual instincts (which have hitherto
been engaged in auto-erotic activities) in order to obtain a
love-object; and he begins by taking himself, his own body,
as his love-object, and only subsequently proceeds from
this to the choice of some person other than himself as
his object. This half-way phase between auto-erotism and
object-love may perhaps be indispensable normally; but

it appears that many people linger unusually long in this condition, and that many of its features are carried over by them into the later stages of their development. What is of chief importance in the subject's self thus chosen as a love object may already be the genitals. The line of development then leads on to the choice of an external object with similar genitals - that is, to homosexual object-choice - and thence to heterosexuality. People who are manifest homosexuals in later life have, it may be presumed, never emancipated themselves from the binding condition that the object of their choice must possess genitals like their own; and in this connection the infantile sexual theories which attribute the same kind of genitals to both sexes exert much influence.

[1] Sadger (1910) and Freud (1910*c*).

[2] Freud, *Three Essays on the Theory of Sexuality* (1905*d*).

After the stage of heterosexual object-choice has been reached, the homosexual tendencies are not, as might be supposed, done away with or brought to a stop; they are merely deflected from their sexual aim and applied to fresh uses. They now combine with portions of the ego-instincts and, as 'attached' components, help to constitute the social instincts, thus contributing an erotic factor to friendship and comradeship, to *esprit de corps* and to the love of mankind in general. How large a contribution is in fact derived from erotic sources (with the sexual aim inhibited) could scarcely be guessed from the normal social relations of mankind.

But it is not irrelevant to note that it is precisely manifest homosexuals, and among them again precisely those that set themselves against an indulgence in sensual acts, who are distinguished by taking a particularly active share in the general interests of humanity - interests which have themselves sprung from a sublimation of erotic instincts.

In my *Three Essays on the Theory of Sexuality* I have expressed the opinion that each stage in the development of psychosexuality affords a possibility of 'fixation, and thus of a dispositional point. People who have not freed themselves completely from the stage of narcissism - who, that is to say, have at that point a fixation which may operate as a disposition to a later illness - are exposed to the danger that some unusually intense wave of libido, finding no other outlet, may lead to a sexualization of their social instincts and so undo the sublimations which they had achieved in the course of their development. This result may be produced by anything that causes the libido to flow backwards (i.e. that causes a 'regression'): whether, on the one hand, the libido becomes collaterally reinforced owing to some disappointment over a woman, or is directly dammed up owing to a mishap in social relations with other men - both of these being instances of 'frustration'; or whether, on the other hand, there is a general intensification of the libido, so that it becomes too powerful to find an outlet along the channels which are already open to it, and consequently bursts through its banks at the weakest spot. Since our analyses show that paranoics *endeavour to protect themselves against any such sexualization of their social instinctual cathexes*, we are driven to suppose that the weak spot in their development is to be looked for somewhere between the stages of auto-erotism, narcissism and homosexuality, and that their disposition to illness (which may perhaps be susceptible of more precise definition) must be located in that region. A similar disposition would have to be assigned to patients suffering from Kraepelin's dementia praecox or (as Bleuler has named it) *schizophrenia*; and we shall hope later on to find clues which will enable us to trace back the differences between the two disorders (as regards both the form they take and the course they run) to corresponding differences in the patients' dispositional fixations.

In taking the view, then, that what lies at the core of the conflict in cases of paranoia among males is a homosexual wishful phantasy of *loving a man*, we shall certainly not forget that the confirmation of such an important hypothesis can only follow upon the investigation of a large number of instances of every variety of paranoic disorder. We must therefore be prepared, if need be, to limit our assertion to a single type of paranoia. Nevertheless, it is a remarkable fact that the familiar principal forms of paranoia can all be represented as contradictions of the single proposition: '*I* (a man) *love him* (a man)'; and indeed that they exhaust all the possible ways in which such contradictions could be formulated.

The proposition 'I (a man) love him' is contradicted by:

(*a*) Delusions of *persecution*; for they loudly assert: 'I do not *love* him - I *hate* him.'

This contradiction, which must have run thus in the unconscious,[1] cannot, however, become conscious to a paranoiac in this form. The mechanism of symptom-formation in paranoia requires that internal perceptions - feelings - shall be replaced by external perceptions. Consequently the proposition 'I hate him' becomes transformed by *projection* into another one: '*He hates* (persecutes) *me*, which will justify me in hating him.' And thus the impelling unconscious feeling makes its appearance as though it were the consequence of an external perception:

'I do not *love* him - I *hate* him, because HE PERSECUTES ME.'

Observation leaves room for no doubt that the persecutor is some one who was once loved.

(*b*) Another element is chosen for contradiction in *erotomania*, which remains totally unintelligible on any other view:

'I do not love *him* - I love *her*.'

90

And in obedience to the same need for projection, the proposition is transformed into: 'I observe that *she* loves me.'

'I do not love *him* - I love *her*, because SHE LOVES ME.'

Many cases of erotomania might give an impression that they could be satisfactorily explained as being exaggerated or distorted heterosexual fixations, if our attention were not attracted by the circumstance that these infatuations invariably begin, not with any internal perception of loving, but with an external perception of being loved. But in this form of paranoia the intermediate proposition 'I love *her*' can also become conscious, because the contradiction between it and the original proposition is not a diametrical one, not so irreconcilable as that between love and hate: it is, after all, possible to love *her* as well as *him*. It can thus come about that the proposition which has been substituted by projection ('*she loves me*') may make way again for the 'basic language' proposition 'I love *her*'.

¹ Or in the 'basic language', as Schreber would say.

(*c*) The third way in which the original proposition can be contradicted would be by delusions of *jealousy*, which we can study in the characteristic forms in which they appear in each sex.

(α) Alcoholic delusions of jealousy. The part played by alcohol in this disorder is intelligible in every way. We know that that source of pleasure removes inhibitions and undoes sublimations. It is not infrequently disappointment over a woman that drives a man to drink - but this means, as a rule, that he resorts to the public-house and to the company of men, who afford him the emotional satisfaction which he has failed to get from his wife at home. If now these men become the objects of a strong libidinal cathexis in his unconscious, he will ward it off with the third kind of contradiction:

'It is not *I* who love the man - *she* loves him', and he suspects the woman in relation to all the men whom he himself is tempted to love.

Distortion by means of projection is necessarily absent in this instance, since, with the change of the subject who loves, the whole process is in any case thrown outside the self. The fact that the woman loves the men is a matter of external perception to him; whereas the facts that he himself does not love but hates, or that he himself loves not this but that person, are matters of internal perception.

(β) Delusions of jealousy in women are exactly analogous.

'It is not *I* who love the women - *he* loves them.' The jealous woman suspects her husband in relation to all the women by whom she is herself attracted owing to her homosexuality and the dispositional effect of her excessive narcissism. The influence of the time of life at which her fixation occurred is clearly shown by the selection of the love-objects which she imputes to her husband; they are often old and quite inappropriate for a real love relation - revivals of the nurses and servants and girls who were her friends in childhood, or sisters who were her actual rivals.

[(*d*)] Now it might be supposed that a proposition consisting of three terms, such as '*I love him*', could only be contradicted in three different ways. Delusions of jealousy contradict the subject, delusions of persecution contradict the verb, and erotomania contradicts the object. But in fact a fourth kind of contradiction is possible - namely, one which rejects the proposition as a whole:

'*I do not love at all - I do not love any one.*' And since, after all, one's libido must go somewhere, this proposition seems to be the psychological equivalent of the proposition: 'I love only myself.' So that this kind of contradiction would give us megalomania, which we may regard as a *sexual overvaluation of the ego* and may thus set beside the overvaluation of the love-object with which we are already familiar.[1]

It is of some importance in connection with other parts of the theory of paranoia to notice that we can detect an element of megalomania in most other forms of paranoic disorder. We are justified in assuming that megalomania is essentially of an infantile nature and that, as development proceeds, it is sacrificed to social considerations. Similarly, an individual's megalomania is never so vehemently suppressed as when he is in the grip of an overpowering love:

Denn wo die Lieb' erwachet, stirbt

das Ich, der finstere Despot.[2]

After this discussion of the unexpectedly important part played by homosexual wishful phantasies in paranoia, let us return to the two factors in which we expected from the first to find the distinguishing marks of paranoia, namely, the mechanism *by which the symptoms are formed* and the mechanism *by which repression is brought about*.

We certainly have no right to begin by assuming that these two mechanisms are identical, and that symptom-formation follows the same path as repression, each proceeding along it, perhaps, in an opposite direction. Nor does there seem to be any great probability that such an identity exists. Nevertheless, we shall refrain from expressing any opinion on the subject until we have completed our investigation.

[1] *Three Essays on the Theory of Sexuality.* The same view and the same formulation will be found in the papers by Abraham and Maeder to which I have already referred.

[2] From the *Ghazals* of Muhammad ibn Muhammad (Jālal al-Din) *Rumi*, translated by Rückert.

[For when the flames of love arise,

Then Self, the gloomy tyrant, dies.]

Psycho-Analytic Notes on an Autobiographical Account of a Case of Paranoia (Dementia Paranoides)

The most striking characteristic of symptom-formation in paranoia is the process which deserves the name of *projection*. An internal perception is suppressed, and, instead, its content, after undergoing a certain kind of distortion, enters consciousness in the form of an external perception. In delusions of persecution the distortion consists in a transformation of affect; what should have been felt internally as love is perceived externally as hate. We should feel tempted to regard this remarkable process as the most important element in paranoia and as being absolutely pathognomonic for it, if we were not opportunely reminded of two things. In the first place, projection does not play the same part in all forms of paranoia; and, in the second place, it makes its appearance not only in paranoia but under other psychological conditions as well, and in fact it has a regular share assigned to it in our attitude towards the external world. For when we refer the causes of certain sensations to the external world, instead of looking for them (as we do in the case of others) inside ourselves, this normal proceeding, too, deserves to be called projection. Having thus been made aware that more general psychological problems are involved in the question of the nature of projection, let us make up our minds to postpone the investigation of it (and with it that of the mechanism of paranoic symptom-formation in general) until some other occasion; and let up now turn to consider what ideas we can collect on the subject of the mechanism of repression in paranoia. I should like to say at once, in justification of this temporary renunciation, that we shall find that the manner in which the process of repression occurs is far more intimately connected with the developmental history of the libido and with the disposition to which it gives rise than is the manner in which symptoms are formed.

In psycho-analysis we have been accustomed to look upon pathological phenomena as being derived in a general way from repression. If we examine what is spoken of as 'repression' more closely, we shall find reason to split the process up into three phases which are easily distinguishable from one another conceptually.

(1) The first phase consists in *fixation*, which is the precursor and necessary condition of every 'repression'. Fixation can be described in this way. One instinct or instinctual component fails to accompany the rest along the anticipated normal path of development, and, in consequence of this inhibition in its development, it is left behind at a more infantile stage. The libidinal current in question then behaves in relation to later psychological structures like one belonging to the system of the unconscious, like one that is repressed. We have already shown that these instinctual fixations constitute the basis for the disposition to subsequent illness, and we may now add that they constitute above all

the basis for the determination of the outcome of the third phase of repression.

(2) The second phase of repression is that of repression proper - the phase to which most attention has hitherto been given. It emanates from the more highly developed systems of the ego - systems which are capable of being conscious - and may in fact be described as a process of 'after-pressure'. It gives an impression of being an essentially active process, while fixation appears in fact to be a passive lagging behind. What undergo repression may either be the psychical derivatives of the original lagging instincts, when these have become reinforced and so come into conflict with the ego (or ego-syntonic instincts), or they may be psychical trends which have for other reasons aroused strong aversion. But this aversion would not in itself lead to repression, unless some connection had been established between the unwelcome trends which have to be repressed and those which have been repressed already. Where this is so, the repulsion exercised by the conscious system and the attraction exercised by the unconscious one tend in the same direction towards bringing about repression. The two possibilities which are here treated separately may in practice, perhaps, be less sharply differentiated, and the distinction between them may merely depend upon the greater or lesser degree in which the primarily repressed instincts contribute to the result.

(3) The third phase, and the most important as regards pathological phenomena, is that of failure of repression, of *irruption*, of *return of the repressed*. This irruption takes its start from the point of fixation, and it implies a regression of the libidinal development to that point.

We have already alluded to the multiplicity of the possible points of fixation; there are, in fact, as many as there are stages in the development of the libido. We must be prepared to find a similar multiplicity of the mechanisms of repression proper and of the mechanisms of irruption (or of symptom-formation), and we may already begin to suspect that it will not be possible to trace back all of these multiplicities to the developmental history of the libido alone.

It is easy to see that this discussion is beginning to trench upon the problem of 'choice of neurosis', which, however, cannot be taken in hand until preliminary work of another kind has been accomplished. Let us bear in mind for the present that we have already dealt with fixation, and that we have postponed the subject of symptom-formation; and let us restrict ourselves to the question of whether the analysis of Schreber's case throws any light upon the mechanism of repression proper which predominates in paranoia.

At the climax of his illness, under the influence of visions which were 'partly of a terrifying character, but partly, too, of an indescribable grandeur' (73), Schreber became convinced of the imminence of a great catastrophe, of the end of the world. Voices told him that the work of the past 14,000 years had now come to nothing, and that the earth's allotted span was only 212 years more (71); and during the last part of his stay in Flechsig's clinic he believed that that period had already elapsed. He himself was 'the only real man left alive', and the few human shapes that he still saw - the doctor, the attendants, the other patients - he explained as being 'miracled up, cursorily improvised men'. Occasionally the converse current of feeling also made itself apparent: a newspaper was put into his hands in which there was a report of his own death (81); he himself existed in a second, inferior shape, and in this second shape he one day quietly passed away (73). But the form of his delusion in which his ego was retained and the world sacrificed proved itself by far the more powerful. He had various theories of the cause of the catastrophe. At one time he had in mind a process of glaciation owing to the withdrawal of the sun; at another it was to be destruction by an earthquake, in the occurrence of which he, in his capacity of 'seer of spirits', was to act a leading part, just as another seer was alleged to have done in the Lisbon earthquake of 1755 (91). Or again, Flechsig was the culprit, since through his magic arts he had sown fear and terror among men, had wrecked the foundations of religion, and spread abroad general nervous disorders and immorality, so that devastating pestilences had descended upon mankind (91). In any case the end of the world was the consequence of the conflict which had broken out between him and Flechsig, or, according to the aetiology adopted in the second phase of his delusion, of the indissoluble bond which had been formed between him and God; it was, in fact, the inevitable result of his illness. Years afterwards, when Dr. Schreber had returned to human society, and could find no trace in the books, the musical scores, or the other articles of daily use which fell into his hands once more, of anything to bear out his theory that there had been a gap of vast duration in the history of mankind, he admitted that his view was no longer tenable: '. . . I can no longer avoid recognizing that, externally considered, everything is as it used to be. Whether, nevertheless, there may not have been a profound internal change is a question to which I shall recur later.' (84-5.) He could not bring himself to doubt that during his illness the world had come to an end and that, in spite of everything, the one that he now saw before him was a different one.

A world-catastrophe of this kind is not infrequent during the agitated stage in other cases of paranoia.[1] If we base ourselves on our theory of libidinal cathexis, and if we follow the hint given by Schreber's view of other people as being 'cursorily improvised men', we shall not find it difficult to explain these catastrophes.[2] The patient has withdrawn from the people in his environment and from the external world generally the libidinal cathexis which he has hitherto directed on to them. Thus everything has become indifferent and irrelevant to him, and has to be explained by means of a secondary rationalization as being 'miracled up, cursorily improvised'. The end of the world is the projection of this internal catastrophe; his subjective world has come to an end since his withdrawal of his love from it.[3]

After Faust has uttered the curses which free him from the world, the Chorus of Spirits sings:

Weh! Weh!

Du hast sie zerstört,

die schöne Welt,

mit mächtiger Faust!

sie stürzt, sie zerfällt!

Ein Halbgott hat sie zerschlagen!

.   .   .   .   .   .

Mächtiger

der Erdensöhne,

Prächtiger

baue sie wieder,

in deinem Busen baue sie auf![4]

And the paranoic builds it again, not more splendid, it is true, but at least so that he can once more live in it. He builds it up by the world of his delusions. *The delusional formation, which we take to be the pathological product, is in reality an attempt at recovery, a process of reconstruction.* Such a reconstruction after the catastrophe is successful to a greater or lesser extent, but never wholly so; in Schreber's words, there has been a 'profound internal change' in the world. But the human subject has recaptured a relation, and often a very intense one, to the people and things in the world, even though the relation is a hostile one now, where formerly it was hopefully affectionate. We may say, then, that the process of repression proper consists in a detachment of the libido from people - and things - that were previously loved. It happens silently; we receive no intelligence of it, but can only infer it from subsequent events. What forces itself so noisily upon our attention is the process of recovery, which undoes the work of repression and brings back the libido again on to the people it had abandoned. In paranoia this process is carried out by the method of projection. It was incorrect to say that the perception which was suppressed internally is projected outwards; the truth is rather, as we now see, that what was abolished internally returns from without. The thorough examination of the process of projection which we have postponed to another occasion will clear up our remaining doubts on this subject.

[1] An 'end of the world' based upon other motives is to be found at the climax of the ecstasy of love (cf. Wagner's *Tristan und Isolde*); in this case it is not the ego but the single love-object which absorbs all the cathexes directed upon the external world.

² Cf. Abraham (1908) and Jung (1907). Abraham's short paper contains almost all the essential views put forward in the present study of the case of Schreber.

³ He has perhaps withdrawn from it not only his libidinal cathexis, but his interest in general - that is, the cathexes that proceed from his ego as well. This question is discussed below.

⁴ [Woe! Woe!

Thou hast it destroyed,

The beautiful world,

With powerful fist!

In ruins 'tis hurled,

By the blow of a demigod shattered!

.   .   .   .   .

Mightier

For the children of men,

More splendid

Build it again,

In thine own bosom build it anew!]

In the meantime, however, it is a source of some satisfaction to find that our newly acquired knowledge involves us in a number of further discussions.

(1) Our first reflection will tell us that it cannot be the case that this detachment of the libido occurs exclusively in paranoia; nor can it be that, where it occurs elsewhere, it has such disastrous consequences. It is quite possible that a detachment of the libido is the essential and regular

mechanism of every repression. We can have no positive knowledge on that point until the other disorders that are based upon repression have been similarly examined. But it is certain that in normal mental life (and not only in periods of mourning) we are constantly detaching our libido in this way from people or from other objects without falling ill. When Faust freed himself from the world by uttering his curses, the result was not a paranoia or any other neurosis but simply a certain general frame of mind. The detachment of the libido, therefore, cannot in itself be the pathogenic factor in paranoia; there must be some special characteristic which distinguishes a paranoic detachment of the libido from other kinds. It is not difficult to suggest what that characteristic may be. What use is made of the libido after it has been set free by the process of detachment? A normal person will at once begin looking about for a substitute for the lost attachment; and until that substitute has been found the liberated libido will be kept in suspension within his mind, and will there give rise to tensions and colour his mood. In hysteria the liberated libido becomes transformed into somatic innervations or into anxiety. But in paranoia the clinical evidence goes to show that the libido, after it has been withdrawn from the object, is put to a special use. It will be remembered that the majority of cases of paranoia exhibit traces of megalomania, and that megalomania can by itself constitute a paranoia. From this it may be concluded that in paranoia the liberated libido becomes attached to the ego, and is used for the aggrandizement of the ego. A return is thus made to the stage of narcissism (known to us from the development of the libido), in which a person's only sexual object is his own ego. On the basis of this clinical evidence we can suppose that paranoics have brought along with them a *fixation at the stage of narcissism*, and we can assert that the length of *the step back from sublimated homosexuality to narcissism* is a measure of the amount of *regression* characteristic of paranoia.

(2) An equally plausible objection can be based upon Schreber's case history, as well as upon many others. For it can be urged that the delusions of persecution (which were directed against Flechsig) unquestionably made their appearance at an earlier date than the phantasy of the end of the world; so that what is supposed to have been a return of the repressed actually preceded the repression itself - and this is patent nonsense. In order to meet this objection we must leave the high ground of generalization and descend to the detailed consideration of actual circumstances, which are undoubtedly very much more complicated. We must admit the possibility that a detachment of the libido such as we are discussing might just as easily be a partial one, a drawing back from some single complex, as a general one. A partial detachment should be by far the commoner of the two, and should precede a general one, since to begin with

it is only for a partial detachment that the influences of life provide a motive. The process may then stop at the stage of a partial detachment or it may spread to a general one, which will loudly proclaim its presence in the symptoms of megalomania. Thus the detachment of the libido from the figure of Flechsig may nevertheless have been what was primary in the case of Schreber; it was immediately followed by the appearance of the delusion, which brought back the libido on to Flechsig again (though with a negative sign to mark the fact that repression had taken place) and thus annulled the work of repression. And now the battle of repression broke out anew, but this time with more powerful weapons. In proportion as the object of contention became the most important thing in the external world, trying on the one hand to draw the whole of the libido on to itself, and on the other hand mobilizing all the resistances against itself, so the struggle raging around this single object became more and more comparable to a general engagement; till at length a victory for the forces of repression found expression in a conviction that the world had come to an end and that the self alone survived. If we review the ingenious constructions which were raised by Schreber's delusion in the domain of religion - the hierarchy of God, the proved souls, the fore-courts of Heaven, the lower and the upper God - we can gauge in retrospect the wealth of sublimations which were

brought down in ruin by the catastrophe of the general
detachment of his libido.

(3) A third consideration which arises from the views
that have been developed in these pages is as follows. Are
we to suppose that a general detachment of the libido from
the external world would be an effective enough agent
to account for the 'end of the world'? Or would not the
ego-cathexes which still remained in existence have been
sufficient to maintain *rapport* with the external world? To
meet this difficulty we should either have to assume that
what we call libidinal cathexis (that is, interest emanating
from erotic sources) coincides with interest in general, or we
should have to consider the possibility that a very widespread
disturbance in the distribution of libido may bring about a
corresponding disturbance in the ego-cathexes. But these are
problems which we are still quite helpless and incompetent
to solve. It would be otherwise if we could start out from
some well-grounded theory of instincts; but in fact we have
nothing of the kind at our disposal. We regard instinct as
being the concept on the frontier-line between the somatic
and the mental, and see in it the psychical representative of
organic forces. Further, we accept the popular distinction
between ego-instincts and a sexual instinct; for such a
distinction seems to agree with the biological conception
that the individual has a double orientation, aiming
on the one hand at self-preservation and on the other at

the preservation of the species. But beyond this are only hypotheses, which we have taken up - and are quite ready to drop again - in order to help us to find our bearings in the chaos of the obscurer processes of the mind. What we expect from psycho-analytic investigations of pathological mental processes is precisely that they shall drive us to some conclusions on questions connected with the theory of instincts. These investigations, however, are in their infancy and are only being carried out by isolated workers, so that the hopes we place in them must still remain unfulfilled. We can no more dismiss the possibility that disturbances of the libido may react upon the ego-cathexes than we can overlook the converse possibility - namely, that a secondary or induced disturbance of the libidinal processes may result from abnormal changes in the ego. Indeed, it is probable that processes of this kind constitute the distinctive characteristic of psychoses. How much of all this may apply to paranoia it is impossible at present to say. There is one consideration, however, on which I should like to lay stress. It cannot be asserted that a paranoic, even at the height of the repression, withdraws his interest from the external world completely - as must be considered to occur in certain other kinds of hallucinatory psychosis (such a Meynert's amentia). The paranoic perceives the external world and takes into account any alterations that may happen in it, and the effect it makes upon him stimulates him to invent explanatory theories (such as Schreber's 'cursorily improvised men'). It therefore appears to me far more probable that the paranoic's altered relation to the world is to be explained entirely or in the main by the loss of his libidinal interest.

(4) It is impossible to avoid asking, in view of the close connection between the two disorders, how far this conception of paranoia will affect our conception of dementia praecox. I am of opinion that Kraepelin was entirely justified in taking the step of separating off a large part of what had hitherto been called paranoia and merging it, together with catatonia and certain other forms of disease, into a new clinical unit - though 'dementia praecox' was a particularly unhappy name to choose for it. The designation chosen by Bleuler for the same group of forms - 'schizophrenia' - is also open to the objection that the name appears appropriate only so long as we forget its literal meaning. For otherwise it prejudices the issue, since it is based on a characteristic of the disease which is theoretically postulated - a characteristic, moreover, which does not belong exclusively to that disease, and which, in the light of other considerations, cannot be regarded as the essential one. However, it is not on the whole of very great importance what names we give to clinical pictures. What seems to me more essential is that paranoia should be maintained as an independent clinical type, however frequently the picture it offers may be complicated by the presence of schizophrenic features. For, from the standpoint

of the libido theory, while it would resemble dementia praecox in so far as the repression proper would in both disorders have the same principal feature - detachment of the libido, together with its regression on to the ego - it would be distinguished from dementia praecox by having its dispositional fixation differently located and by having a different mechanism for the return of the repressed (that is, for the formation of symptoms). It would seem to me the most convenient plan to give dementia praecox the name of *paraphrenia*. This term has no special connotation, and it would serve to indicate a relationship with paranoia (a name which cannot be changed) and would further recall hebephrenia, an entity which is now merged in dementia praecox. It is true that the name has already been proposed for other purposes; but this need not concern us, since the alternative applications have not passed into general use.

Abraham has very convincingly shown [1] that the turning away of the libido from the external world is a particularly clearly-marked feature in dementia praecox. From this feature we infer that the repression is effected by means of detachment of the libido. Here once more we may regard the phase of violent hallucinations as a struggle between repression and an attempt at recovery by bringing the libido back again on to its objects. Jung, with extraordinary analytic acumen, has perceived that the deliria[2] and motor stereotypes occurring in this disorder are the residues of former object-cathexes, clung to with great persistence. This attempt at recovery, which observers mistake for the disease itself, does not, as in paranoia, make use of projection, but employs a hallucinatory (hysterical) mechanism. This is one of the two major respects in which dementia praecox differs from paranoia; and this difference can be explained genetically from another direction. The second difference is shown by the outcome of the disease in those cases where the process has not remained too restricted. The prognosis is on the whole more unfavourable than in paranoia. The victory lies with repression and not, as in the former, with reconstruction. The regression extends not merely to narcissism (manifesting itself in the shape of megalomania) but to a complete abandonment of object-love and a return to infantile auto-erotism. The dispositional fixation must therefore be situated further back than in paranoia, and must lie some where at the beginning of the course of development from auto-erotism to object-love. Moreover, it is not at all likely that homosexual impulsions, which are so frequently - perhaps invariably - to be found in paranoia, play an equally important part in the aetiology of that far more comprehensive disorder, dementia praecox.

¹ In the paper already quoted.

² [In French and German psychiatry the word 'delirium' is often used of delusional states.]

Psycho-Analytic Notes on an Autobiographical Account of a Case of Paranoia (Dementia Paranoides)

Our hypotheses as to the dispositional fixations in paranoia and paraphrenia make it easy to see that a case may begin with paranoic symptoms and may yet develop into a dementia praecox, and that paranoid and schizophrenic phenomena may be combined in any proportion. And we can understand how a clinical picture such as Schreber's can come about, and merit the name of a paranoid dementia, from the fact that in its production of a wishful phantasy and of hallucinations it shows paraphrenic traits, while in its exciting cause, in its use of the mechanism of projection, and in its outcome it exhibits a paranoid character. For it is possible for several fixations to be left behind in the course of development, and each of these in succession may allow an irruption of the libido that has been pushed off - beginning, perhaps, with the later acquired fixations, and going on, as the illness develops, to the original ones that lie nearer the starting-point. We should be glad to know to what conditions the relatively favourable issue of the present case is due; for we cannot willingly attribute the whole responsibility for the outcome to anything so casual as the 'improvement due to change in domicile',[1] which set in after the patient's removal from Flechsig's clinic. But our insufficient acquaintance with the intimate circumstances of the history of the case makes it impossible to give an answer to this interesting question. It may be suspected, however, that what enabled Schreber to reconcile himself to his homosexual phantasy, and so made it possible for his illness to terminate in something approximating to a recovery, may have been the fact that his father-complex was in the main positively toned and that in real life the later years of his relationship with an excellent father had probably been unclouded.

[1] Cf. Riklin (1905).

Since I neither fear the criticism of others nor shrink from criticizing myself, I have no motive for avoiding the mention of a similarity which may possibly damage our libido theory in the estimation of many of my readers. Schreber's 'rays of God', which are made up of a condensation of the sun's rays, of nerve fibres, and of spermatozoa, are in reality nothing else than a concrete representation and projection outwards of libidinal cathexes; and they thus lend his delusions a striking conformity with our theory. His belief that the world must come to an end because his ego was attracting all the rays to itself, his anxious concern at a later period, during the process of reconstruction, lest God should sever His ray-connection with him, - these and many other details of Schreber's delusional structure sound almost like endopsychic perceptions of the processes whose existence I have assumed in these page as the basis of our explanation of paranoia. I can nevertheless call a friend and fellow-specialist to witness that I had developed my theory of paranoia before I became acquainted with the contents of Schreber's book. It remains for the future to decide whether there is more delusion in my theory than I should like to admit, or whether there is more truth in Schreber's delusion than other people are as yet prepared to believe.

Lastly, I cannot conclude the present work, which is once again only a fragment of a larger whole, without foreshadowing the two chief theses towards the establishment of which the libido theory of the neuroses and psychoses is advancing: namely, that the neuroses arise in the main from a conflict between the ego and the sexual instinct, and that the forms which the neuroses assume retain the imprint of the course of development followed by the libido - and by the ego.

POSTSCRIPT
(1912)

In dealing with the case history of Senatspräsident Schreber I purposely restricted myself to a minimum of interpretation and I feel confident that every reader with a knowledge of psycho-analysis will have learned from the material which I presented more than was explicitly stated by me, and that he will have found no difficulty in drawing the threads closer and in reaching conclusions at which I no more than hinted. By a happy chance the same issue of this periodical as that in which my own paper appeared showed that the attention of some other contributors had been directed to Schreber's autobiography, and made it easy to guess how much more material remains to be gathered from the symbolic content of the phantasies and delusions of this gifted paranoic.[1]

Since I published my work upon Schreber, a chance acquisition of knowledge has put me in a position to appreciate one of his delusional beliefs more adequately, and to recognize the wealth of its bearing upon *mythology*. I mentioned on p. 2425 the patient's peculiar relation to the sun, and I was led to explain the sun as a sublimated 'father-symbol'. The sun used to speak to him in human language and thus revealed itself to him as a living being.

Schreber was in the habit of abusing it and shouting threats at it; he declares, moreover, that when he stood facing it and spoke aloud, its rays would turn pale before him. After his 'recovery' he boasts that he can gaze at it without any difficulty and without being more than slightly dazzled by it, a thing which would naturally have been impossible for him formerly.[2]

It is to this delusional privilege of being able to gaze at the sun without being dazzled that the mythological interest attaches. We read in Reinach[3] that the natural historians of antiquity attributed this power to the eagle alone, who, as a dweller in the highest regions of the air, was brought into especially intimate relation with the heavens, with the sun, and with lightning.[4] We learn from the same sources, moreover, that the eagle puts his young to a test before recognizing them as his legitimate offspring. Unless they can succeed in looking into the sun without blinking they are thrown out of the eyrie.

[1] Cf. Jung (1911, 164 and 207); and Spielrein (1911, 350).

[2] See the footnote to page 139 of Schreber's book.

[3] Reinach (1905-12, 3, 80), quoting Keller (1887).

[4] Representations of eagles were set up at the highest points of temples, so as to serve as 'magical' lightning-conductors. (Cf. Reinach, loc. Cit.)

There can be no doubt about the meaning of this animal myth. It is certain that this is merely ascribing to animals something that is a hallowed custom among men. The procedure gone through by the eagle with his young is an *ordeal*, a test of lineage, such as is reported of the most various races of antiquity. Thus the Celts living on the banks of the Rhine used to entrust their new-born babies to the waters of the river, in order to ascertain whether they were truly of their own blood. The clan of Psylli, who inhabited what is now Tripoli, boasted that they were descended from snakes, and used to expose their infants to contact with them; those who were true-born children of the clan were either not bitten or recovered rapidly from the effects of the bite.[1] The assumption underlying these trials leads us deep into the *totemic* habits of thought of primitive peoples. The totem - an animal, or a natural force animistically conceived, to which the tribe traces back its origin - spares the members of the tribe as being its own children, just as it itself is honoured by them as being their ancestor and is spared by them. We have here arrived at the consideration of matters which, as it seems to me, may make it possible to arrive at a psycho-analytic explanation of the origins of religion.

The eagle, then, who makes his young look into the sun and requires of them that they shall not be dazzled by its light, is behaving as though he were himself a descendant of the sun and were submitting his children to a test of their ancestry. And when Schreber boasts that he can look into the sun unscathed and undazzled, he has rediscovered the mythological method of expressing his filial relation to the sun, and has confirmed us once again in our view that the sun is a symbol of the father. It will be remembered that during his illness Schreber gave free expression to his family pride,[2] and that we discovered in the fact of his childlessness a human motive for his having fallen ill with a feminine wishful phantasy. Thus the connection between his delusional privilege and the basis of his illness becomes evident.

[1] For lists of references see Reinach, loc. cit. and ibid., 1, 74.

[2] The Schrebers are 'members of the highest nobility of Heaven' (24). - '*Adel*' is the attribute of an '*Adler*'. ['*Adel*' means 'nobility' or 'noble'. '*Adler*' means 'eagle' or 'noble (person)'.]

This short postscript to my analysis of a paranoid patient may serve to show that Jung had excellent grounds for his assertion that the mythopoeic forces of mankind are not extinct, but that to this very day they give rise in the neuroses to the same psychical products as in the remotest past ages. I should like to take up a suggestion that I myself made some time ago,[1] and add that the same holds good of the forces that construct religions. And I am of opinion that the time will soon be ripe for us to make an extension of a thesis which has long been asserted by psycho-analysts, and to complete what has hitherto had only an individual and ontogenetic application by the addition of its anthropological counterpart, which is to be conceived phylogenetically. 'In dreams and in neuroses', so our thesis has run, ' we come once more upon the *child* and the peculiarities which characterize his modes of thought and his emotional life.' 'And we come upon the *savage* too,' we may now add, 'upon the *primitive* man, as he stands revealed to us in the light of the researches of archaeology and of ethnology.'

[1] 'Obsessive Acts and Religious Practices' (1907*b*).

CPSIA information can be obtained
at www.ICGtesting.com
Printed in the USA
LVHW012053050820
662472LV00008B/1423